Write Papers

2nd Edition

By
Ron Fry

CAREER PRESS
180 Fifth Avenue
P.O. Box 34
Hawthorne, NJ 07507
1-800-CAREER-1
201-427-0229 (outside U.S.)
FAX: 201-427-2037

WRITE PAPERS (2ND ED.)

ISBN 1-56414-081-4, $6.95

Cover design by A Good Thing, Inc.

Printed in the U.S.A. by Book-mart Press

To order this title by mail, please include price as noted above, $2.50 handling per order, and $1.00 for each book ordered. Send to: Career Press, Inc., 180 Fifth Ave., P.O. Box 34, Hawthorne, NJ 07507.

Or call toll-free 1-800-CAREER-1 (Canada: 201-427-0229) to order using VISA or MasterCard, or for further information on books from Career Press.

Library of Congress Cataloging-in-Publication Data

Fry, Ronald W.
   Write papers / by Ron Fry. -- 2nd ed.
     p.   cm.
   Includes index.
   ISBN 1-56414-081-4 : $6.95
   1. Report writing. 2. Research. I. Title.
LB1047.3.F79   1994
371.3'028'13--dc20   94-5490
                                  CIP

Comments

STUDY SMARTER, NOT HARDER!

Ron Fry's **HOW TO STUDY** *Program,* the best-selling and most acclaimed study series of all time, has sold more than 1,000,000 copies in four years. It is used in colleges, high schools and junior highs and by parents and students throughout the world. And Ron has appeared on hundreds of radio and TV shows and countless newspaper and magazine articles and profiles again and again to trumpet his message: Study Smarter, Not Harder!

Here are just a few of the things reviewers have said about *Ron Fry's* **HOW TO STUDY** *Program:*

"These books belong in every secondary library and perhaps in every English classroom. **Highly recommended.**"
— *Library Materials Guide*, Christian Schools International

"Fry's **lively style of writing** makes the book **very useful**."
— *Library Journal*

"Fry has an **appealing, down-to-earth style** that makes this text **accessible and practical.** A regular classroom teacher could extract pertinent lessons to prepare all students to be more successful scholars. The Series would also be appropriate for self-study by college students."
— *Intervention* magazine

"...**approachable, chatty and interactive.** Fry speaks directly to the reader in an **encouraging and sympathetic** fashion it will benefit students from high school age on up."
— *Kliatt Young Adult Paperback Guide*

"...I really liked *How to Study.* **A great gift** for any student."
— *Bookviews*

"Wow! This guy makes sense, he's funny, and he is easy to read. I got the feeling this approach might even work for me!"
— Virginia Meldrum, owner of the Owl's Tree bookstore

"This series **could be useful in resource rooms, in a regular classroom setting or as a self-study guide.**"
— Learning Disabilities Association of Canada

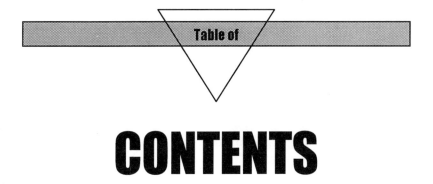

CONTENTS

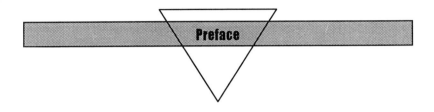

WHO IS THIS BOOK *REALLY* FOR?

All of the now-seven titles in my **HOW TO STUDY Program** were originally written, or so I thought at the time, for high school students. But over the years I've discovered that the students buying these books are either already in college (which says wonderful things about the preparation they got in high school), in junior high (which says something much more positive about their motivation and, probably, eventual success) or returning to college (about whom more later).

Many of you reading this are adults. Some of you are returning to school. And some of you are long out of school but have figured out that if you could learn *now* the study skills your teachers never taught you, you'll do better in your careers. (Especially if you knew how to write that attention-getting memo or raise-making report.)

All too many of you are parents with the same lament: "How do I get Johnny to do better in school? His idea of researching a paper is reading the appropriate *Classics Illustrated* comic."

I want to briefly take the time to address every one of the audiences for this book and discuss some of the factors particular to each of you:

If you're a high school student

You should be particularly comfortable with both the language and format of the book—its relatively short sentences and paragraphs, occasionally humorous (hopefully) headings and subheadings, a reasonable but certainly not outrageous vocabulary. I wrote it with you in mind! While you may have prepared book reports, projects and short papers in junior high or middle school, you can count on being assigned 10- to 15-page papers with some regularity during high school. (And if you're planning to go on to college, I guarantee you *must* master these skills.)

If you're a junior high school student

You are trying to learn how to study at *precisely* the right time. Sixth, seventh and eighth grades—before that sometimes cosmic leap to high school—is without a doubt the period in which all these study skills should be mastered, since doing so will make high school not just easier but a far more positive and successful experience. Although written for high school-level readers, if you're serious enough about studying to be reading this book, I doubt you'll have trouble with the concepts or the language. While those hefty 10- or 15-page papers are probably a couple of grades away, learning to use the library, prepare better book reports and mastering good note-taking and organizational skills now can only help when that first term paper *is* assigned.

If you're a "traditional" college student...

...somewhere in the 18 to 25 age range, I would have hoped you had already mastered most if not all of the basic study skills, especially reading and writing. Since you haven't, please make learning, using and mastering all of the study skills covered in my **HOW TO STUDY** *Program* an absolute priority. Do not pass "Go." Do not go on a date. Take the time to learn these skills now. You may have been able to slide by in high school by copying whole sections of obscure reference books whenever a paper was due, betting your grade that your teacher wouldn't recognize your source. I suspect you'll find college to be another world, one in which you'll find yourself "sliding" down the grading curve unless you get serious about your study skills...right now!

If you're the parent of a student of any age

You must be convinced of one incontestable fact: It is highly unlikely that your child's school is doing anything to teach him or her how to study. Yes, of course they should. Yes, I know that's what you thought you paid taxes for. Yes, yes, yes. But, but, but—believe me, *they're not doing it.*

How do I know? For one thing, in thousands of interviews on radio, TV and in the print media, my publisher has allowed me to make the same offer: They will give any teacher or school administrator wishing to use any or all of the books in my **HOW TO STUDY** *Program* one *free* book for every one they purchase. That's right, buy 10, get 10 free. Buy 100, get 100 free.

Write Papers

There are three teachers out there—all three spending *their own money*, mind you—who have taken me up on that offer. Says something about priorities, doesn't it?

I also spend a lot of time talking to students and visiting schools. And the lack of study skills training is woefully obvious, whether the school is in the poorest section of town or the richest, in the inner city or suburban heaven, public or private, elementary, junior high or high school.

Writing papers (along with note-taking and time management, I think) is one of the skills many teachers seem to assume students can simply learn by osmosis. While term papers are virtually automatic in every English, history and social studies class from ninth grade up, I've yet to meet many teachers who take the time to teach a good note-taking system, for example, or simple techniques to organize a jumble of notes into a coherent, clearly written paper.

Don't for a minute underestimate the importance of *your* commitment to your child's success: Your involvement in your child's education is absolutely essential to his or her eventual success. Surprisingly enough, the results of every study done in the last two decades about what affects a child's success in school concludes that only one factor *overwhelmingly* affects it, every time: parental involvement. Not the size of the school, the money spent per pupil, the number of language labs, how many of the student body go on to college, how many great teachers there are (or lousy ones). All factors, yes. *But none as significant as the effect **you** can have.*

So please, take the time to read this book (and all of the others in the series, but especially **How to Study)** yourself. Learn what your kids *should* be learning. (And which of the other five subject-specific books in the series your child needs the most.)

And you can help tremendously, *even if you were not a great student yourself, even if you never learned great study skills.* You can learn now together with your child—not only will it help him or her in school, it will help *you* on the job, whatever your job.

Even if you think you need help only in a single area—or two or three—don't use only the specific book in my program that highlights that subject. Read **How to Study** first, *all the way through.* First of all, it will undoubtedly help you increase your mastery of skills you thought you already had. And it will cover those you need help with in a more concise manner. With that background, you will get *more* out of whichever of the other six books you use.

Presuming you need all the help all seven books can give you, what order should you read them in? Aside from reading **How to Study** first—all the way through—I don't think it matters. All of the study skills are interrelated, so practicing one already helps you with the others. If pushed, however, I will admit that I would probably suggest **Improve Your Reading** and **Manage Your Time** be the first two books you study. The former because reading is the basis of every other study skill, the latter because organization is the foundation on which the study pyramid is erected. After that, take your pick!

If you're a nontraditional student

If you're going back to high school, college or graduate school at age 25, 45, 65 or 85—you probably need the help these seven books offer more than anyone! Why? Because the longer you've been out of school, the more likely you don't remember what you've forgotten. And you've forgotten what you're supposed to remember! As much as I emphasize that it's rarely too early to learn good study habits, I must also emphasize that it's never too *late*.

Why you're holding a new edition

I first wrote **How to Study** in 1988, convinced that schools were doing a lousy job of teaching kids how to study—synonymous, to me, with teaching them how to *learn*—and that no one was picking up the slack. (I was also convinced—and still am—that most kids wanted *desperately* to learn but would, without some help, find it easier to fail. And failure, once welcomed, is a nasty habit to break.)

Published in 1989, most bookstores wedged one or two copies of **Study** in between the hundreds of phone book-sized test prep volumes. Career Press wasn't a big enough publisher to convince the "chains"—Waldenbooks, Barnes & Noble, B. Dalton—to stock it in any quantity or rich enough to spend any money promoting it.

Despite these obstacles, tens of thousands of people who obviously needed **How to Study** ferreted out copies wherever they lurked. In 1990, the chains—who *are* smart enough to at least spot a winner the *second* time around—bought 6-copy "prepacks" and gave the book a little more prominence. (Meaning you didn't have to get a hernia removing other books to find a copy of **Study**.) Career Press sent me around the country to appear on radio and TV, including CNN. And hundreds of newspapers and magazines noticed what we were doing and started writing about **How to Study**. (The fact that test scores had declined for the hundred-fortieth year in a row or so probably had something to do with this, but who am I to quibble with the attention?)

In 1991, *booksellers* started calling to say they hoped I was planning some follow-up books to **Study**. And hundreds of parents and students wrote or called to indicate they needed more help in some specific areas. ***Ron Fry's* HOW TO STUDY *Program*** was born, featuring a second edition of ***Study*** and four new books—***Improve Your Reading, Manage Your Time, Take Notes and Write Papers***—that delved even deeper into those critical study skills. That year I spent more time on the phone doing radio shows than I did, I think, with my wife and 2-year-old daughter.

In 1992, I added two more volumes—***"Ace" Any Test*** and ***Improve Your Memory***, both of which were pretty much written in response to readers' letters. Surprisingly, ***Test*** and ***Memory*** quickly became the second- and third-biggest sellers of the seven books in the series, beaten only by ***How to Study.*** Evidently, my readers knew darned well what they were requesting.

By the way, in both 1992 and 1993, I added mightily to my Frequent Flyer accounts while talking to people nationwide about studying. I wound up visiting 50 cities, some twice, and appearing on more TV and radio shows than are listed in your daily newspaper.

The result of all this travel was twofold: First, sales of all seven books have skyrocketed, in part because of the chance I've been given to talk about them on so many shows and in so many news-papers and magazines. Second, I got to meet and talk with tens of thousands of students and parents, many of whom confirmed the ongoing need for these books *because very little has changed since I first wrote* **How to Study** *some six years ago.*

Test scores of every kind are lower today than they were then. More and more students are dropping out or, if they *do* manage to graduate high school, are finding they are not equipped to do *any*thing. And more and more parents are frus-trated by their children's inability to learn and their schools' seeming inability to teach.

With so much new feedback, it was time to revise all seven books, all of which are being published in time for "back to school" in 1994. In every book, I've included additional topics and expanded on others. I've changed some examples, simplified some, eliminated some. I've rewritten sentences, paragraphs or entire sections that students seemed to be struggling with. Most importantly, I've tried to reflect my new understanding of just who is reading these books—"traditional" students, their parents *and* nontraditional (i.e. older, perhaps much older) students, many of those self-same parents—and write in such a way to include all three audiences.

A couple of caveats

Before we get on with all the tips and techniques you need to produce A-plus papers and applause-generating oral reports, let me make two important points about all seven study books.

First, I believe in gender equality, in writing as well as in life. Unfortunately, I find constructions such as "he and she," "s/he," "womyn" and other such stretches to be sometimes painfully awkward. I have therefore attempted to sprinkle pronouns of both genders throughout the text. Some teachers, for example, are "he," some are "she." I think this is preferable to using the masculine pronoun throughout but proclaiming one's feminist leanings or to creating so-called "gender-neutral" words or phrases that I find inhibit the "flow" I try to achieve in my writing.

Second, you will find many pieces of advice, examples, lists and other words, phrases and sections spread throughout two or more of the seven books. Certainly *How to Study*, which is an overview of all the study skills, necessarily contains, though in summarized form, some of each of the other six books. But there are discussions of note-taking in *Write Papers* and *Take*

Notes, tips about essay tests in *"Ace" Any Test* and *Write Papers*, time management techniques in *Manage Your Time* and *Improve Your Reading*.

The repetition is unavoidable. While I urge everyone to read all seven books in the series, but especially *How to Study*, they *are* seven individual books. Many people only buy one of them. Consequently, I must include in each the pertinent material *for that topic*, even if that material is then repeated in a second or even a third book. As I will point out throughout all the books, these study skills are intimately interrelated. You can't discuss writing papers without covering taking notes for those papers. Or improving your reading without discussing how to take notes from textbooks.

In many cases, not only is the same topic covered, but it is covered in the same language or uses the same example. If I am particularly happy with the way I covered a subject in one book, I have not gone out of my way to rewrite a sentence, paragraph or, for that matter, a whole section just to say it "differently" in another. (Besides, for those who follow my advice and work with all seven books, the repetition of some of the same important points can only help them learn it more quickly and easily.)

That said, I can guarantee that the nearly 1,000 pages of my *HOW TO STUDY Program* contain the most wide-ranging, comprehensive and complete system of studying ever published. I have attempted to create a system that is usable, that is useful, that is practical, that is learnable. One that *you* can use—whatever your age, whatever your level of achievement, whatever your IQ—to start doing better in school *immediately*.

I hope after reading these books you'll agree I've succeeded.

I'm sure after reading these books that *you'll* succeed.

Ron Fry
May, 1994

TAMING THE DREADED "R" MONSTER

It's going to happen.

There you'll be, sitting quietly in class, contemplating the weekend to come, minding your own business.

Suddenly, without even a warning, your teacher will announce that your next assignment is...to write a Research Paper.

There's no getting around it. At some time during your years as a student, you'll have to face the dreaded "R" monster.

Nothing strikes more fear in the hearts of students everywhere. The thought of spending hours in the library digging up information...writing a long, detailed report...typing footnotes. For heaven's sake—if it's not enough to bring on actual terror, it certainly qualifies for mild panic!

"How will I get it all done?" you think. "Where do I start?" And, no doubt, "Why *me?*"

The fact that you picked up this book means you already have encountered the "R" monster, or expect to meet up with it all too soon. (I'm not naive enough to believe that you would actually *want* to write a research paper *just for the heck of it*—although that *would* be a valuable exercise.)

So let me reassure you right off: You will get it done. You will get a great grade on it. You will even learn a few things along the way. How? With the help of this book. I've been there. (And since I'm still writing after all these years, I'm *still* there!) I'll show you my "tricks of the trade," every step of the way.

Step-by-step to success

A Buddhist saying proclaims that "the journey of a thousand miles begins with a single step." Well, so does the process of writing your research paper. The secret is to take things one step at a time. By breaking your assignment—no matter how huge or time-consuming a project—into a series of small steps, you'll turn a conceivably immense undertaking into a series of very manageable jobs.

First, in Chapter 1, you'll learn about the different elements that make up a research paper. I'll show you how to put together a work schedule *and* give you some tips on time management.

In Chapter 2, I'll help you decide on a specific topic...and show you the kinds of topics to avoid like sour milk. I'll also show you how to develop a specific research angle or research argument—your *thesis*—and produce a preliminary outline for your paper.

Then, in Chapters 3, 4 and 5, we'll spend some time in the library. You'll learn where to look for reference materials, a great system for keeping track of those you use, and a special note-taking system. You'll quickly be transformed into a more efficient, organized researcher—and get *more* done in *less* time.

In Chapters 6 and 7, you'll begin the actual writing of your paper. I'll show you some tricks that will help you organize it, some tips on overcoming writer's block and a checklist to make sure you avoid plagiarizing. By the end of Chapter 7, you'll already have written a rough draft.

In Chapter 8, we'll discuss the various methods you can use to document your sources of information—*when* you must document a source and *how* to do it.

Next, in Chapter 9, we'll edit your rough draft. You'll learn special strategies that will make your writing better, smoother, clearer.

You'll learn the ins and outs of putting together a bibliography—a list of the reference materials you used to write your paper—in Chapter 10. I'll give you the lowdown on all the rules you need to follow.

In Chapter 11, you'll learn some super proofreading tricks so you catch *every* typographical error and spelling mistake in your paper. And *voilà!* You'll be on your way to class, finished masterpiece in hand!

Two sections new to this edition: In Chapter 12, I've summarized the advice from *"Ace" Any Test* regarding essay tests. Since my advice for such a test is to "treat it like writing a paper," a short section on essays seemed appropriate to this book. In this chapter I've also added a section on oral reports which, though previously written for *How to Study,* also belongs in this book.

Finally, in Chapter 13, I discuss Attention Deficit Disorder (ADD), hyperactivity and the combination condition, ADHD. I have, as a matter of fact, included some version of this chapter in new editions of five of my books (all but *"Ace" Any Test* and *How to Study* itself). While these problems concern a minority of you, it is a large minority and a very concerned one. Parents of children with ADD were usually the first callers on any radio show on which I appeared. Because so many of the study skills I discuss are much more difficult to master for students with ADD, these parents always urged me to address *their* children and point out the tips and techniques *they* needed to learn to succeed in school. With the help of my good friend Thom Hartmann, author of **Attention Deficit Disorder: A Different Perception**, I believe Chapter 13 offers the help these parents asked for.

You'll thank them later—really!

Yes, you're right. Doing a research paper means a lot of work. But the payoff is great, too. In addition to the obvious benefit—learning a lot about your research subject—you'll develop important skills every step of the way. You'll learn, for example:

1. How to track down information about *any* subject.
2. How to sort through that information and come to a conclusion about your subject.
3. How to prepare an organized, in-depth report.
4. How to communicate your ideas clearly and effectively.

Once you develop these skills, you own them.
You'll be able to apply them in *all* your high-school or college classes. They'll come in handy not only when you prepare other research papers, but also when you tackle smaller writing assignments, such as essays and oral reports.

When you graduate, these same skills will help you get ahead in the work world—the ability to analyze a subject and communicate through the written word are keys to success, no matter what career you choose.

Your teacher really didn't ask you to write a research paper just to make your life miserable. Of all the things you'll learn in school, the skills you acquire as we produce your research paper will be among the most valuable.

How to use this book

The steps I outline throughout this book are somewhat flexible. After you've "notched your pen" with one or two papers, you may want to adapt these steps a bit to fit your personal work style.

That's fine, just *don't skip any step altogether*. You may not understand the benefits of a particular step until you're further along in the process. So trust me. If you skip a step, you'll inevitably make your life more difficult in the long run.

Let's get started

Writing a research paper takes time, serious thought and effort. It is *not* easy. I can't change that any more than I can change your teacher's mind about assigning the paper in the first place.

But I *can* tell you that if you follow the steps outlined in this book, you'll find that the "R" monster is not such a terrifying creature after all. And I can guarantee that you will learn some things along the way that will stay with you for the rest of your life.

It won't be painless, but at least the operation will be a success!

Chapter One

A LOOK AT THE JOB(S) AHEAD

You may be only writing *one* paper, but there are actually *three* different jobs ahead of you:

First, you must be an *objective reporter*—you'll dig up all the facts you can about your subject, gathering statistics, historical data, first-person accounts and more.

You will read reference books, newspaper stories, magazine articles, scholarly journals and other materials, watch a relevant video or film, even interview a live expert or two.

Your job is to find out the truth, to gather data with an unbiased eye.

You can't discard or ignore information just because it doesn't fit into the neat framework your personal opinions and expectations have constructed.

Second, you must be a *detective.*

Like a scientist evaluating the results of an experiment, you must review the evidence, decide what it does and doesn't mean, and draw the obvious (and, perhaps, not-so-obvious) conclusions.

Third, you must be an *author,* ready to share your new-found knowledge.

Having sifted through reams of information, you will write a cogent, well-thought-out, in-depth report, telling your readers what you have learned.

This is an exciting process—where else can you play three such different roles in a matter of weeks?—but one that demands some organization and adherence to a short but vitally important list of rules.

Four "Always", one "Never"

Let's start with the fundamental rules that need to be emblazoned on your wall:

1. *Always* follow your teacher's directions to the letter
2. *Always* hand in your paper on time
3. *Always* hand in a clean and clear copy of your paper
4. *Always* keep at least one copy of every paper you write
5. *Never* allow a single spelling or grammatical error in your papers

You wanted it *type*written?

Your teacher's directions may include:

• A general subject area from which topics should be chosen—"some aspect of Kennedy's presidency," "an

18th-century invention," "a short story by Washington Irving," etc.

- Specific requirements regarding format—typed, double-spaced, include title page, do not include title page, etc.
- Suggested length—10-15 typewritten pages.
- Other requirements—turn in general outline before topic is approved; get verbal okay on topic before proceeding; don't include quotes (from other works) longer than a single paragraph; other idiosyncrasies of your own teachers.

Whatever his or her directions, *follow them to the letter.* Some high school teachers may forgive you your trespasses, but I have known college professors who simply refused to accept a paper that was not prepared as they instructed—and gave the poor but wiser student an "F" for it (without even *reading* it).

If you are unsure of a specific requirement or if the suggested area of topics is unclear, it is *your* responsibility to talk to your teacher and clarify whatever points are confusing you.

It is also not a bad idea to choose two or three topics you'd like to write about and seek his or her preliminary approval, especially if the assignment seems particularly vague.

So then my little brother erased my hard drive...

There is certainly no reason, short of catastrophic illness or life-threatening emergency, for you to *ever* be late with an assignment. Barring those, there is rarely an acceptable excuse for being late. Again, some teachers will simply refuse to accept a paper that is late and give you an "F" for your efforts. At best, they will accept it but mark you down, perhaps turning an "A" paper into a "B"...or worse.

Teachers don't read tea stains

Teachers have to read a lot of papers and shouldn't be faulted for being human if, after hundreds of pages, they come upon your wrinkled, tea-stained, pencil-written tome and get a bit discouraged. Nor should you be surprised if they give you a lower grade than the content might merit *just because the presentation is so poor.*

I am not advocating that you emphasize form over substance. Far from it—the content is what the teacher is looking for, and he or she will primarily be basing your grade on *what* you write. But presentation *is* important, teachers are only human (really!) and you can't fault them for trying to teach *you* to take pride in your work. So follow these simple rules:

- Never handwrite your paper.

- If you're using a word processor or word-processing program on your computer, use a new ribbon in your dot matrix printer and/or check the toner cartridge of your laser printer. If you type (or have someone else type) your paper, use clean white bond and (preferably) a new carbon ribbon so that the images are crisp and clear.

- Unless otherwise instructed, always double-space your paper. And leave adequate margins all around.

- Use a simple typeface that is clear and easy-to-read; avoid those that are too big—stretching a five-page paper to 10—or too small and hard to read.

- And never use a fancy italic, modern or any other ornate or hard-to-read typeface for the entire paper.

What are your old papers trying to tell you?

There should be a number of helpful messages in your returned papers, which is why it's so important to retain them. What did your teacher have to say? Are her comments applicable to the paper you're writing now—poor writing, lack of organization, lack of research, bad transitions between paragraphs, poor grammar or punctuation, misspellings? The more such comments—and, one would expect, the lower the grade— the more extensive the "map" your teacher has given you for your *next* paper, showing you right where to "locate" your A-plus.

If you got a low grade but there aren't any comments, shouldn't you have asked the teacher why you got such a poor grade? You may get the comments you need to make the next paper better. You will also be showing the teacher you actually care, which could help your grade the next time around.

Create a work schedule

Here are the steps that, with some minor variations along the way, are common to virtually any written report or paper:

1) Finalize your topic

2) Carry out initial library research

3) Prepare a general outline

4) Do detailed library research

5) Prepare detailed outline (from note cards)

6) Write your first draft

7) Do additional research (if necessary)

Write Papers

8) Write your second draft

9) Spell-check and proofread

10) Have someone *else* proofread

11) Produce a final draft

12) Proofread one last time

13) Turn it in and collect your A-plus

Doing all these tasks efficiently and effectively requires careful timing and planning. After all, this isn't the only assignment, and may not even be the only paper, you have to get done in a short amount of time.

So get out your calendar and mark the date your paper is due. How many weeks till then? Four? Six? Ten? Plan to spend at least half of that time on research, the rest on writing. (In general, research should take up from one-half to three-quarters of your entire schedule for a paper.)

Now, block out set periods of time during each week to work on your paper. Try to schedule large chunks of time—two, three hours or more at a shot—rather than many short periods. Otherwise, you'll spend most of your time "reviewing" where you left off and repeating steps unnecessarily.

As you make up your work schedule, set deadlines for completing the general steps of your paper-writing process. See the example on the next page.

Of course, I can't tell you exactly how much time to set aside for each step, because I don't know any of the specifics about your paper—how long it's supposed to be, how complex the topic, etc.—or how fast you work. I *can* tell you that you should plan on consulting and/or taking notes from at least 10 different books, articles or other reference materials. (Your

Week 1:	Decide on topic and "angle" of your paper.
Week 2:	Make list of reference materials.
Weeks 3/4:	Read reference materials; take notes.
Weeks 5/6:	Do detailed outline; write first draft.
Week 7:	Edit paper; prepare bibliography.
Week 8:	Proofread paper; type final copy.

teacher or subject may demand even *more;* I doubt you'll need fewer.) And you should plan on writing two or three drafts of your paper before you arrive at the final copy.

Refer to your work schedule often, and adjust your pace if you find yourself lagging behind.

The more time you have to complete a project, the easier it is to procrastinate about dealing with it, even to putting off identifying the steps and working them into your regular schedule. If you find yourself leaving such long-term projects to the last week, schedule the projects furthest away—the term paper due in three months, the oral exam 10 weeks from now—*first.* Then, trick yourself—schedule the completion date at least seven days prior to the actual turn-in date, giving yourself a one-week cushion for life's inevitable surprises. (Just try to forget you've used this trick. Otherwise, you'll be like the perennial latecomer who set his watch 15 minutes fast in an effort to finally get somewhere on time. Except that he always reminded himself to add 15 minutes to the time on his wrist, defeating the whole purpose.)

If you only had the time...

Mastering "time management" does not require the brain of a rocket scientist—it just means *making the most of your time.* And that means planning ahead—for example, instead of making 15 short trips to the library, plan five or six extended research periods. You'll save travel time and footwork and get a lot more done in the same period of time.

Be prepared. Stock up on pencils, typewriter ribbons, computer disks and any other work supplies you need. Otherwise, you may find yourself running to the store at midnight in search of an elusive printer ribbon or laser cartridge.

And *stay* organized. Keep all materials related to your paper in a separate notebook or file. No messy piles of work scattered here and there, just waiting to be lost or thrown away by mistake.

For a look at "everything you ever wanted to know" about time management, pick up a copy of *Manage Your Time*, another of the seven recently revised books in my **HOW TO STUDY** *Program.*

And don't procrastinate!

Do not, I repeat, do *not* put off doing your research paper until the last minute—or even until the last week! If you do, you will make your task much more difficult. And probably wind up with a lousy paper, too.

Start working on your assignment now. *Right* now.

Chapter Two

DEVELOPING YOUR BATTLE PLAN

You're ready to take the first and conceivably most important step on the road to your A-plus research paper: deciding on a subject.

Once you've chosen a *general* area of study, you must target a *specific* topic or research question. Then, you need to come up with a general outline—a sketchy blueprint of your paper.

In this chapter, I'll help you complete all three tasks.

Choosing your topic

In some cases, your teacher will assign your topic. In others, your teacher will assign a general area of study, and you'll have the freedom to pick a specific topic.

With freedom sometimes comes danger—give this decision long and careful thought. Pick the wrong topic, and you can write yourself right into disaster.

I'm not implying that you should pick the simplest topic you can find—simple topics often lead to simply awful papers. But there are definitely some pitfalls you must avoid.

Danger #1: Thinking too big

You need to write a 15-page paper for your American history class and decide your topic will be "America's Role in World War II."

Whoa, Nelly! Think about it: Can you really cover a topic that broad in *15* pages? Not unless you simply rehash the high points, *à la* your third-grade history book. You could write volumes on the subject (people have) and still have plenty left to say!

Instead, you need to focus on a particular, limited aspect of such a broad subject or attack it from a specific angle. Rather then "America's Role in World War II," how about "The Role of the Women Air Force Service Pilots in World War II"?

Remember, your job is to prepare an *in-depth* report about your subject. Be sure you can do that in the number of pages your teacher has requested.

Danger #2: Thinking too small

By the same token, you must not focus too narrowly. Choose a subject that's too limited, and you might run out of things to say on the second page of your paper. "The Design of the Women Air Force Service Pilots' Insignia" might make an interesting one- or two-page story, but it won't fill 10 or 15 pages...even with *really* wide margins.

Hint: If you can't find a single *book* on your supposed topic, rethink it! While there's nothing wrong with choosing a topic that can be researched via magazine articles, the newspaper, monographs and the like, why make your research so difficult if you don't have to?

Danger #3: Trodding the lonesome trail

Pick a topic that's too obscure, and you may find that little or no information has been written about it. In which case, you will have to conduct your own experiments... interview your own research subjects...and come up with your own, original data. That is, of course, how scientists forge new pathways into the unknown. But I'm guessing that you have neither the time, desire nor experience to take a similar start-from-scratch approach.

(Take it from someone who's done this more than once—it may be wonderfully creative and a lot of fun to work in such original areas, but it can also be frustrating and stressful. And don't underestimate the reaction of your teacher, who may well wish for something a little easier to grade than some far-reaching new theory he or she really needs to think about. I got a "C" on the best paper I think I ever wrote. The grad student grading it came right out and told me since he couldn't "check" my ideas—there was nothing published to support my inter-pretation—he couldn't give me a better grade. I think that attitude is absurd—and that the "C" was, too—but suggest you keep it in mind.)

The point is: Make sure that there is enough research material available about your topic. And make sure that there are enough *different* sources of material—different authors, dif-ferent books, etc.—so you can get a well-rounded view of your subject (and not be forced for lack of other material to find ways to make somebody else's points sound like your own).

Make a possibilities list

Taking all of the above into consideration, do a little brainstorming now about possible topics for your paper. Don't stop with the first idea—come up with several different possibilities.

In fact, put this book down and go make a list of three or four potential topics right now.

Do some preliminary research

Got your list? Then get thee to a library. You need to do a little advance research.

Scan your library's card-catalog index or computer listings, the *Readers' Guide to Periodical Literature* and other publication indexes. How many books and articles have been written about each topic on your "possibilities" list? Read a short background article or encyclopedia entry about each topic.

By the time you leave the library, you should have a general understanding of each of your potential subjects. You also should know whether you'll have trouble finding information about any topic on your list. If so, eliminate it.

And the winner is (drum roll, please)...

With any luck at all, you should be left with at least one topic that looks like a good research subject. If two or more topics passed your preliminary-research test, pick the one that interests you most.

You're going to spend a lot of time learning about your subject. There's no rule that says you can't enjoy it!

Develop a temporary thesis

Once you have chosen the topic for your paper, you must develop a *temporary thesis.*

What's a *thesis?* The word "thesis" is a relative of "hypo-thesis"—and means about the same thing: the central argument you will attempt to prove or disprove in your paper. It is the conclusion—based upon your research—you draw about your subject.

A thesis is not the same thing as a *topic.* Your topic is what you study; your thesis is the conclusion you draw from that study.

A *thesis statement* is a one-sentence summary of your thesis, summing up the main point of your paper.

Suppose you decided that the topic of your paper will be "The Role of the Women Air Force Service Pilots in World War II." At the end of your research, you have concluded that these pilots played a very valuable role in the war effort. Your thesis statement, then, might be:

> The Women Air Force Service Pilots played an important role in World War II.

In your paper, you would try to prove this thesis, explaining why the contributions of the pilots were so important.

Temporary means just that

Note that word *temporary.* No matter how good it looks to you now, your temporary thesis may *not* wind up being your final thesis. Because you haven't completed all your research yet, you can only come up with a "best-guess" thesis at this point.

You may find out during your research that your temporary thesis is all wet. If that's the case, you will revise it, perhaps even settling on a thesis that's the exact opposite of your first! In fact, you may revise your thesis *several* times during the course of your research.

If a temporary thesis doesn't spring easily to mind—and it probably won't—sit back, and do some more brainstorming. Ask yourself questions like:

- "What's special or unusual about _____?" (Fill in the blank with your topic.)
- "How is _____ related to events in the past?"
- "What impact has ____ made on society?"
- "What would I like the world to know about ____?"
- "What questions do I have about _____?"

The answers to these and similar questions should lead you to several good thesis ideas. If you find yourself needing more information about your topic to answer these questions, go back to the library and do a bit more reading.

Ask your instructor

Some teachers require you to submit your thesis statement for their approval prior to beginning your paper. Even if this is *not* required, getting your instructor's opinion is always a good idea. He or she will help you determine whether your thesis argument is on target, and, if not, perhaps how to fix it.

Create a temporary outline

Once you have developed your temporary thesis, think about how you might approach the subject in your paper. Jot down the various issues you plan to investigate. Then, come up with a brief, temporary outline of your paper, showing the order in which you might discuss those issues.

Let's suppose your temporary thesis was: "Even though they served as civilians, the Women Air Force Service Pilots of World War II deserved to be given official status as veterans."

Based on what you learned in your preliminary research, your temporary outline might look like this:

A. Why civilian women pilots entered the war
B. The type and number of women who participated
C. Their qualifications and training
D. Their missions and contributions
E. The military vs. civilian status question
F. The disbanding of the group
G. The fight to be recognized as veterans

Don't worry too much about this outline—it will be brief, at best. It's simply a starting point for your research, a plan of attack.

But don't skip this step, either. As you'll find out in later chapters, it will be a big help in organizing your research findings.

Chapter Three

RESEARCH: THE HUNT FOR MATERIALS

You've accomplished a lot so far: You've determined your topic of study. You've developed a temporary thesis. And you've created a temporary outline for your paper. Congratulations!

Now it's time to begin your research in earnest.

We're going to tackle this initial information hunt in two phases. First, you'll come up with a list of all the books, magazines and other research materials you want to consult.

Then, you'll sit down and do the actual reading and note-taking.

In Chapter 4, I'll show you a time-saving way to compile and organize your reading list. And in Chapter 5, I'll teach you an efficient way to take notes.

But first, you need to learn where and how to locate the many different kinds of research materials you can consult.

Into the library

The obvious place to begin your hunt for research materials is the library. Today's libraries offer an amazing variety of resources—learn how to tap into their gold mine of information and you'll be much richer. If you have gotten this far in life *without* being introduced to library basics, just ask your librarian for help. (As a matter of fact, even if you consider yourself something of a library expert, always ask your librarian for help! Make the "information" desk a regular hangout. Tell the librarians what you're working on—they'll invariably know the best sources of information and where to find them.)

Most libraries are divided into reading rooms, restricted collections and unrestricted book stacks. Unrestricted book stacks are those through which anyone using the library can wander, choosing books to use while in the library or, if allowed, to take home. Restricted areas generally include any special collections of rare books, those open only to scholars or to those with particular credentials, either by library rule or by order of whoever donated the collection (and, often, the room housing it) to the library. In some libraries, *all* book stacks are closed, and *all* books must be obtained from a librarian.

Most libraries contain both *circulating materials*—those books and other items you may check out and take home with you—and *noncirculating material*—those that must be used only in the library. All fiction, general nonfiction and even most "scholarly" titles will usually be found in the first group. Reference material, periodicals and books in special collections are usually in the second.

At most libraries, many of those old, familiar library tools—like the trusty card catalog—have been replaced by computerized systems. These can be a little intimidating for first-time users, but they are great time-savers. Again, don't be shy about asking for help. Your librarian will be happy to show you how to make the computers work their magic.

How your library is organized

To provide organization and facilitate access, most small and academic libraries utilize the Dewey Decimal Classification System, which uses numbers from 000 to 999 to classify all material by subject matter. It begins by organizing all books into 10 major groupings:

000 - 099	General
100 - 199	Philosophy
200 - 299	Religion
300 - 399	Social Sciences
400 - 499	Language
500 - 599	Science
600 - 699	Useful Arts
700 - 799	Fine Arts
800 - 899	Literature
900 - 999	History

Given the millions of books available in major libraries, just dividing them into these 10 groups would still make it quite difficult to find a specific title. So each of the 10 major groupings is further divided into 10 and each of these now one hundred groups is assigned to more specific subjects within each large group. For example, within the Philosophy classification (100), 150 is psychology and 170 is ethics. Within the history classification (900), 910 is travel and 930 is ancient history.

There is even further subdivision. Mathematics is given its own number in the 500 (Science) series—510. But specific subjects within mathematics are further classified: 511 is arithmetic; 512, algebra, and so on.

Finally, to simplify your task even more, the last two digits in the Dewey code signify the type of book:

01	Philosophy of
02	Outlines of
03	Dictionary of
04	Essays about
05	Periodicals on
06	Society transactions and proceedings
07	Study or teaching of
08	Collections
09	History of

If your library doesn't use the Dewey system, it probably is organized according to the Library of Congress System, which uses letters instead of numbers to denote major categories:

A General works (encyclopedias and other reference)

B Philosophy, Psychology and Religion

C History: Auxiliary sciences (archeology, genealogy, etc.)

D History: General, non-American

E American history (general)

F American history (local)

G Geography/Anthropology

H Social sciences (sociology, business, economics)

J Political sciences

K Law

L Education

M Music
N Fine arts (art and architecture)
P Language/Literature
Q Sciences
R Medicine
S Agriculture
T Technology
U Military science
V Naval science
Z Bibliography/Library science

Beyond the encyclopedia

When you were younger, you probably relied solely on the encyclopedias in your school library when you had to write a report. Sorry, but those simpler, easier days are gone for good.

Yes, you may want to read encyclopedias to get a general overview of your topic. But you need to turn to other sources for more detailed information. You need to read books written by experts in the field you're researching, and magazine and newspaper articles about every aspect of your subject.

Why stop there? Pamphlets...brochures...government documents...specialized anthologies...films and videos...these are just some of the other possible sources of information for your paper.

Where to look for materials

How do you find out whether anyone has written a magazine or newspaper article about your topic? How do you know if there are any government documents or pamphlets that might be of help? How do you locate those written-by-the-experts reference books?

You look in your library's publication indexes, which list all of the articles, books and other materials that have been published and/or are available in your library. Most are arranged alphabetically by subject.

Be sure to look under more than one subject heading when you search for reference materials. For example, if we were looking for resources for our World War II paper, we might look under "Women in Aviation," "Veterans—Women," and "World War II."

Some of the major publication indexes are listed below. There are others—ask your librarian for suggestions.

1. ***The Card Catalog:*** This is a list of all the books in your library. (Although many libraries now store it on computer, it's still often called a card catalog because it used to be kept on index cards.) Books are indexed in three different ways: by subject, author and title.

2. ***Newspaper Indexes:*** Several large-city newspapers provide an indexed list of all articles they have published. Your library may even have past issues of one or more available on microfiche.

3. ***Periodical Indexes:*** To find out if any magazine articles have been published on your subject, go to a periodical index. *The Readers' Guide to Periodical Literature,* which indexes articles published in the most popular American magazines, may be one with which you're familiar.

4. ***Vertical File:*** Here's where you'll find pamphlets and brochures.

5. ***U.S. Documents Monthly Catalog:*** Useful for locating government publications.

Other ideas

When you're making up your list of possible reference materials (which you'll learn how to do in the next chapter), you also may want to check the following:

1. *Special Anthologies, Almanacs and Encyclopedias:* Providing more in-depth information than general encyclopedias, these are entire series devoted exclusively to specific topics.
2. *Association Directories:* An association or organization related to your topic can be one of your most valuable sources of information. Often, such organizations have a historian who can provide you with extensive literature—or, better yet, the names of experts whom you might interview! You can find their names and addresses here.

Your approach to research

All of us who have become familiar with the wonders of the library have probably developed our own approach to enjoying them and using them most efficiently. My own experience emphasizes what may be the obvious: Getting the right start is all-important. Since I try to keep from being overwhelmed with material, I start any research working with the broadest outlines or topics (and the broadest resources) and wind my way down the ladder, getting more and more specific in topic and sources as I go.

Let's assume, for example, that you have to prepare a report on the current political situation of South Africa as it specifically relates to the end of apartheid. Here's how you might approach the task:

1. **Go to a dictionary** and look up the term apartheid. Make certain you have a firm understanding of what this word means before you proceed any further!

2. Consult any one of the numerous leading **encyclopedias** you will find in your library—Britannica, Americana, Collier's, World Book, etc. Here you'll find an overview and historical prospective on the subject of these special racial laws. Encyclopedic entries are usually the most comprehensive and concise you will find. They cover so much territory and are so (relatively) up to date that they are an ideal "big-picture" resource.

3. With overview in hand, you can start consulting the **major indexes and directories** your library has to develop a list of more specific resources. Obviously, the entries in these major resources can then be directly consulted—specific issues of *The New York Times* on microfilm, periodicals at the periodicals desk, etc. And, of course, your card catalog or computer terminal will spew out listings for hundreds of other books on the general issue of apartheid or any related subject it touches (which you learned about while skimming pertinent sections of the above general resources)—The African National Congress, Nelson and Winnie Mandela, de Klerk, black homelands, Desmond Tutu, Kwazulu, Natal, the Inkatha Freedom Party, etc.

In one brief tour of your library's resources, you'll easily discover and know how to obtain more material than you would need to write a book on virtually any one of the subtopics, let alone a report encompassing all of them.

Write Papers

What if you're uncomfortable in the library? An infrequent user? Or simply find it a confusing place that's more trouble than it's worth?

As I've emphasized, developing *any* habit is just a matter of practice. The more you use the library, the more comfortable you will become using it. And, of course, the more books you will become comfortable with. In a very short time, you will have your own "personal" list of resources that you start with whenever you receive an assignment.

If you want the library to become like a second home, its every shelf a familiar friend, why not go to work there? Many libraries, smaller ones in particular, often offer opportunities for paid and volunteer work. Even if you work for free, this is an excellent way to learn the ins and outs of your library.

Many of you might not use the library as much as you should (or even would like) because it's just a confusing series of catacombs. The more comfortable you are—the more you know about the materials it contains and how to locate and use them—the more you will *want* to be there.

And the more help you will be able to obtain from this great resource that's just waiting to welcome you!

On to chapter 4.

CREATING A WORKING BIBLIOGRAPHY

Working bibliography? "Ugh," you think, "sounds complicated."

Relax. Remember what I told you in Chapter 3—the first step of your research is to put together a list of books, magazines, pamphlets, etc., you want to read. "Working bibliography" is simply a fancy name for that list.

There are two steps involved. First, you'll create bibliography cards for each source of information you want to review. Then, you'll transfer all the information from your bibliography cards to a single list—your working bibliography.

This two-step method has been around since someone wrote the first research paper, and with good reason: It works! It helps you conduct your research in an organized, efficient manner *and* makes preparing your final bibliography easier.

In other words, this is one of those great time-saving tools that I promised to show you!

This is not a complicated job, but it is an important one. So follow my instructions to the letter.

Essential ingredients: 3 x 5 index cards

To create your working bibliography, you'll need a supply of 3 x 5 index cards. You can buy these for next to nothing at most dime stores, bookstores and office stores. (You'll also use index cards when you take notes for your paper, so buy a big batch now. A few hundred cards ought to suffice.)

While you're stocking up on index cards, pick up one of those little boxes designed to hold the cards. Put your name, address and phone number on the box. If you lose it, some kind stranger may return it. If not, after you have to duplicate all your work, I guarantee you will never lose one again.

Step 1: Create your bibliography cards

You'll complete the first step of the bibliography two-step at the library. Take your index cards, a couple of pens or pencils—and this book, of course.

Start a systematic search for any materials that might have information related to your paper. Look through the indexes we covered in Chapter 3 and any other indexes your librarian recommends.

When you find a book, article or other resource that looks promising, take out a blank note card. On the front of the card, write down the following information:

In the upper right-hand corner of the card: The library call number (Dewey decimal number or Library of Congress number), if there is one. Add any other detail that will help you locate the material on the library shelves (e.g. "Science Reading Room," "Reference Room," "Microfiche Periodicals Room").

On the main part of the card: The author's name, if given—last name first, first name, middle name or initial. Then the title of the article, if applicable, in quotation marks. Then the name of the book, magazine, newspaper or other publication—underlined.

Add any details you will need if you have to find the book or article again, e.g.:

- Date of publication
- Edition—e.g., "third (1990) edition" for a book; "morning edition" for a newspaper.
- Volume number
- Page numbers on which the article or information appears

In the upper left-hand corner of the card: Number it. The first card you write will be #1, the second, #2, and so on. If you happen to mess up and skip a number somewhere along the line, don't worry. It's only important that you assign a different number to each card.

At the bottom of the card: If you're going to be working in more than one library, write the name of the library. Also write down the name of the index in which you found the resource, in case you need to refer to it again.

Do this for *each* potential source of information you find. *And put only one resource on each card.*

Some experts in the research-paper business have different ideas about what goes where on bibliography cards. It's not really important—if you prefer to put the elements of your card in some different order, it's okay.

Write Papers

Just be sure that you're consistent, so you'll know what's what later on. And leave some room on the card—you'll be adding more information when you actually get the reference material in your hands.

Sample Bibliography Card For A Book

(1)   315.6
Main Reading Room

Halloran, Sally

The Life and Times of Bob Smith.
(see esp. pp. 43-48)

Card Catalog
Main Street Library

Sample Bibliography Card For A Magazine Article

(2)   Periodical Room

Arenas, George
"The Life and Times of Bob Smith"
Smith Magazine
(April 24, 1989; pp. 22-26)

Readers' Guide
University Library

Sample Bibliography Card For A Newspaper Article

```
(3)                           Microfiche Room

              Ellen, Terry
     "Bob Smith: The New Widget Spinner"
              New York Times
     (June 16, 1976, late edition, p. A12)

           New York Times Index
           Main Street Library
```

Evaluating resources

You may find so many potential resources that you know you won't have time to read them all. If so, concentrate on those that have been published most recently or written by the most respected sources.

However, don't limit yourself *too* much—you should gather information from a wide range of sources. Otherwise, you may wind up learning only one side of the story.

Primary vs. secondary resources

There are two basic types of resources: *primary* and *secondary.*

Primary resources are written by people who *actually witnessed or participated in an event.* When you read a scientist's report about an experiment he has conducted, you are consulting a primary resource.

Secondary resources are written by people *who were not actually present at an event,* but have studied the subject. When you read a book about the 1950s written by someone who was born in 1960, you are learning from a secondary resource.

Obviously, primary resources are likely to be more reliable sources of information. But depending upon your subject, there may not *be* any primary resources available to you.

Step 2: Prepare your working bibliography

When you get home, copy the information from each of your bibliography cards onto a single list. As you do this, follow the bibliography style rules outlined in Chapter 10. (These rules cover bibliographic minutiae—where to put periods, how many spaces to indent lines, etc.) When you've finished your list—your working bibliography—make a photocopy or two. Keep one copy with your research file, another in a safe place in your room or desk.

Although you'll work from your bibliography cards as you conduct your research, your working bibliography is important for two reasons:

1. You'll have a separate record of all the potential re-sources you found. If you lose any of your biblio-graphy cards, you can recreate it easily.

2. You'll be able to use your working bibliography as the basis for your final one.

The final bibliography, a required part of your paper, lists resources from which you gathered information. Your *working* bibliography contains all the resources from which you *might* gather information.

Looks like extra work to me!

Why bother to create all those separate bibliography cards if you're just going to transfer the information to another piece of paper? Can I possibly be wasting your time?

Of course not. It's a matter of convenience and organization.

With index cards, you can organize your list of resources in different ways, just by shuffling the deck.

For example, you might want to start by organizing your cards by resource: magazine articles, encyclopedias, books, newspapers, etc. Then, when you're in the magazine room of the library, you will have a quick and easy way to make sure you read all your magazine articles at the same time. Ditto for your trip to the newspaper reading room, the reference shelf, and so on.

But at some point, you might want to have your list of resources organized in alphabetical order. Or separated into piles of resources you've checked, and those you haven't. No problem: Just shuffle your cards again.

Even with the help of a computer, it would be time-consuming to do all of this on paper. The note-card system is neater and more efficient. And that's the key to getting your work done as quickly and painlessly as possible!

Chapter Five

PLANNING FOR GOLD

Did you ever dream of sleuthing about like Agatha Christie? Or "breaking" a front-page story like Woodward & Bernstein? If you ever thought being a detective or investigative reporter could be fun, then get ready to have some! It's time to follow up all of those research leads you found, track down the evidence, and uncover the truth, the whole truth and nothing but the truth.

In other words, it's time to start taking notes.

When you write your paper, you'll work from your notes, not the original reference materials. Why? Because it's easier to turn a few cards than flip through hundreds of pages in search of the information you need. Because it's easier than lugging home stacks of heavy books from the library. And because you don't have a choice—many of the materials you may need to consult can't be taken *out* of the library!

In this chapter, I'm going to show you my own special system for taking notes. Master it—it will be a huge help when you sit down to organize and write your paper.

Send for information/schedule interviews

Before you do anything else, send away for anything you want to review that isn't available in your library. If you want to get a brochure from a particular association, for example, order it now. It may take a few weeks for such materials to arrive.

If you're going to interview any experts, schedule interview dates with them. Make up a list of good questions, and buy or borrow a quality tape recorder so you can accurately record your interviewee's comments.

Then hit the books

Set aside solid blocks of time for your library work. And remember: It's better to schedule a handful of extended trips to the library than 15 or 20 brief visits.

When you go to the library, take your bibliography cards, a good supply of blank index cards, your preliminary outline and several pens or pencils.

Your bibliography cards are the map for your information treasure hunt. When you arrive at the library, pull out the first five or six cards, locate the materials listed on them, pick a secluded desk or table and get to work.

When you write your paper, you'll get all the information you need from your notes, rather than from the original sources. Therefore, it's vital that you take careful and complete notes.

What sort of information should you put in your notes? Anything related to your subject and especially to your thesis. This includes:

1. General background information—names, dates, historical data, etc.
2. Research statistics
3. Quotes by experts
4. Definitions of technical terms

You may be used to keeping your notes in a three-ring binder or notepad. I'm going to show you a note-taking system I think is better—you'll record all of your notes on your blank index cards.

As was the case with your bibliography cards, you must follow some specific guidelines to make this method work. You'll want to refer to the guidelines in this chapter often during your first few note-taking sessions. After that, the system will become second nature to you.

Step #1: Complete the bibliography card

Let's say that you have found a reference book that contains some information about your subject. Before you begin taking notes, get out the bibliography card for that book.

First, check that all of the information on your card is correct. Is the title exactly as printed on the book? Is the author's name spelled correctly?

Next, add any other information you will need to include in your final bibliography. The type of information you need to put on your bibliography card depends on two factors: 1) The type of reference material and 2) the bibliography format you are required to use.

Various authorities have set forth a bewildering array of bibliography rules. While none of them are inherently "right" or "wrong," your individual instructor may not agree with me, so be sure to ask her which rules she wants you to follow.

In this book, we'll cover the bibliography gospel according to the Modern Language Association of America (MLA), one of the most widely accepted authorities on such matters.

Unfortunately, even when using only one set of rules, there are different instructions for different types of materials. You handle a bibliography listing for a magazine article differently than you do for a book, for instance. If I were to show you how to handle all the different types of materials you might encounter, this book would easily be three times as large.

And it would be a waste of time and paper, because there are several books already on the market that *do* show every type of listing under the sun. (The MLA, for example, puts out its own very thorough reference manual.) You may want to consult one of these books if you're working with out-of-the-ordinary types of reference materials. Just make sure that the book that you consult follows the bibliography format your teacher requires.

Because most students rely heavily on books, magazine articles and newspaper articles for research, I'll give you the rules for those materials here.

Bibliography listings typically include three categories of information: the author's name, the title of the work and the publishing information. However, there are lots of little pieces of data that fall within those three categories. Include on your card the following information, in the following order:

For a book:

1. *Name(s) of the author(s)*
2. *Title of the part of the book* used (if the entire book does not deal with your subject), in quotes

3. *Title of the book,* underlined
4. Name of the *editor, translator or compiler*
5. *Edition used,* if more than one edition has been published (If you don't see any information about an edition, assume it's the first.)
6. Number of *volume(s) used,* if more than one
7. Name of the *series,* if the book is part of one
8. *Place of publication, name of the publisher, date of publication*
9. If pertinent information appears in only a small portion of the book, the *page numbers* on which it appears
10. *Supplementary information*—any other details needed to identify the exact book you used (e.g., "Spanish language translation") You generally will find all this information on the book's cover, title page and/or copyright page.

For an article in a magazine or newspaper:

1. *Name(s) of the author(s)*
2. *Title of the article,* in quotation marks
3. *Name of the periodical,* underlined. (If you are working with a newspaper that is not widely known or nationally published, put the name of the city or town in which it is published. For example: The Herald [Lawrence, NJ].)
4. *Series number or name,* if one is given;
5. *Volume number* Include this only if you are working with a scholarly journal. If you're not sure whether a periodical is considered a "scholarly journal," ask your librarian or go ahead and include the volume number just in case.

6. *Date of publication* Include the edition of a newspaper, if there is more than one—i.e., morning or evening edition, early or late edition, etc.
7. The *page numbers* on which the article appears. Include the section letter or number for a newspaper: A8, B12, etc.

For a magazine, look for this information on the front cover and within the article itself. For a newspaper, look at the front page and within the article.

Of course, not every bibliography card will include all of these details. Some books may not have an editor, for example. You don't need to write "no editor" on the card; simply move on to the next applicable piece of information.

Step #2: Fill out your note cards

Once your first bibliography card is finished, set it aside. Get out some blank index cards, and start taking notes from your reference source. Follow these guidelines:

- ***Write one thought, idea, quote or fact on each card.***
  If you encounter a very long quote or string of data, you can write on both the front and back of a card, if necessary. ***But never carry over a note to a second card***.

  What if you simply *can't* fit the piece of information on one card? You're dealing with too much information at once. Break it down into two or more smaller pieces, then put each on a separate card.
- ***Write in your own words.*** Summarize key points about a paragraph or section. Or, restate the material

in your own words. Avoid copying things word for word.

- ***Put quotation marks around any material copied verbatim.*** It's okay to include in your paper a sentence or paragraph written by someone else to emphasize a particular point (providing you do so on a limited basis). But you must copy such statements *exactly as written* in the original—every word, every comma, every period. You also must *always* put such direct quotes within quotation marks.

Add organizational details

As you finish each note card, do the following:

- ***In the upper left-hand corner of the card:*** Write down the resource number of the corresponding bibliography card (from its left-hand corner). This will remind you where you got the information.

- ***Below the resource number:*** Write the page number(s) on which the information appeared.

- Get out your preliminary outline. Under which outline topic heading does the information on your note card seem to fit? Under your "A" heading? Under "C"? ***Jot the appropriate topic letter in the upper right-hand corner of your note card.***

  If you're not sure where the information fits into your outline, put an asterisk (*) instead of a topic letter. Later, when you do a more detailed outline, you can try to fit these "miscellaneous" note cards into specific areas.

- ***Next to the topic letter:*** Jot down a one- or two-word "headline" that describes the information on the card. For example, if your note card contains a statistic on how many women pilots were killed in World War II, your headline might be: "Casualties—Statistics."

- ***When you have finished taking notes from a particular resource,*** put a check mark on the bibliography card. This will let you know that you're done with that resource, at least for now.

Be sure that you transfer information accurately to your note cards. Double-check names, dates and other statistics.

As with your bibliography cards, it's *not* vital that you put each of these elements in the exact places I've outlined above. You just need to be consistent: Always put the page number in the same place, in the same manner. Ditto with the resource number, the topic heading and the headline.

Here's a sample of a completed note card to which you can refer.

Sample Completed Note Card

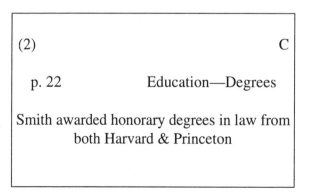

```
(2)                                        C

   p. 22              Education—Degrees

Smith awarded honorary degrees in law from
          both Harvard & Princeton
```

Add your personal notes

Throughout your note-taking process, you may want to make some "personal" note cards—your own thoughts, ideas or impressions about your subject or your thesis.

Perhaps you've thought of a great introduction for your paper. Put it on a card. Or maybe you've thought of a personal experience that relates to your topic. Put it on a card.

Write each thought on a separate note card, just as you have with information you've taken from other resources. And assign your note card a topic heading and mini-headline, too. In the space where you would normally put the number of the re-source, put your own initials or some other symbol. This will remind you that *you* were the source of the information or thought.

Keep an eye out for new resources

When you look up information in one reference book, you'll often find leads to additional resources. Check to see if these resources are on your working bibliography. If not, and you think they are worth consulting, add them. Make up a biblio-graphy card for each new source, too.

Throw away unprofitable leads

If a particular resource doesn't yield any useful information, take the bibliography card for that resource out of your stack. Stick it away in your card file, just in case you want it later.

Or, if you're certain that you won't want to refer back to the resource, throw the bibliography card away altogether. Then scratch the listing from your working bibliography. You don't need to renumber your remaining cards—it doesn't matter if a number is missing.

Why are you doing all this?

Of all the tips you'll learn in this book, this note-taking system is undoubtedly one of the most valuable. In fact, it's one that many *professional* writers swear by (including me).

When you go to write your final bibliography, you'll have all the information you need on your bibliography cards. No trips back to the library to look up bibliography details! Just put your cards in the order that they will appear in your bibliography, and copy the information.

But the biggest benefit of the system is that it helps you organize your findings and makes your writing job easier.

You'll find out *how* easy in the next chapter.

Chapter Six

ORGANIZING YOUR RESEARCH

Your research is done.

Which means—if you managed your time as I suggested earlier—that at least *one-half* of your *paper*—perhaps as much as *three-quarters* of it—is done, even though you've yet to write one word of the first draft. (And you'll soon find you *have* done that already, too!)

You've finished going through all of those reference materials listed in your working bibliography.

You've completed your bibliography cards.

You've uncovered a lot of information about your subject.

And you've taken extensive notes.

It's time to organize your data.

You need to decide if your temporary thesis is still on target, determine how you will organize your paper and create a detailed outline.

Review your thesis statement

Take a close look at your temporary thesis statement.

Does it still make sense, given all the information your research has revealed?

If it doesn't, revise it.

Your research should have led you to *some* conclusion about your subject. This, in turn, should lead you to the final thesis of your paper.

Sort your note cards

Once you have your final thesis, begin thinking about how you will organize your paper. This is where the note-card system you learned in Chapter 5 really pays off. Get out all of your note cards, then:

- Group together all of the cards that share the same outline topic letter (in the upper right-hand corner of each card).

- Put those different groups in order, according to your temporary outline—topic "A" cards on top, followed by topic "B" cards, then topic "C" cards.

- Within each topic group, sort the cards further. Put together all of the cards that share the same "headline"—the two-word title in the upper-right hand corner.

• Go through your miscellaneous topic cards—those marked with an asterisk. Can you fit any of them into your existing topic groups? If so, replace the asterisk with the topic letter. If not, put the card at the very back of your stack.

Decide on the order of your paper

Your note cards now should be organized according to your preliminary outline. Take a few minutes to read through your note cards, beginning at the front of the stack and moving through to the back. *What you are reading is a sketchy draft of your paper*—the information you collected in the order you (temporarily) plan to present it.

Now, consider: Does that order still make sense? Or would another arrangement work better? For example, perhaps you had planned to use chronological order—to tell readers what happened, in the order that it happened. After reviewing your note cards, you may decide that it would be better to take a cause/effect approach—to discuss, one by one, a series of different events and explain the impact of each.

Here are some of the different organizational approaches you might consider for your paper:

1. *Chronological*—discuss events in the order in which they happened (by time or date of occurrence)

2. *Spatial*—present information in geographical or physical order (from north to south, largest to smallest, etc.)

3. *Cause/effect*—one by one, discuss the effects of a series of individual events or actions

4. *Problem/solution*—present a series of problems and possible solutions

5. *Compare/contrast*—discuss the similarities and differences between people, things or events

6. *Order of importance*—discuss the most important aspects of an issue first and continue through to the least important

Your subject matter and your thesis may well determine which of these organizational approaches will work best. If you have a choice of more than one, use the one with which you're most comfortable or that you feel will be easiest for you to write. (Nobody says you *have* to choose the hardest way!) And keep in mind that you can use a *blend* of two approaches—for example, you might mention events in chronological order and then discuss the cause/effect of each.

Resort your cards

If necessary, revise your general outline according to the organizational decision you just made. However, *don't* change the letters that you have assigned to the topics in your outline. If you decide to put topic "B" first in your new outline, for example, keep using the letter "B" in front of it. Otherwise, the topic letters on your note cards won't match those on your outline.

If you revised your outline, reorder your note cards so that they fall in the same order as your new outline.

Now, go through each group of cards that share the same topic letter. Rearrange them so that they, too, follow the organizational pattern you chose.

For an example of how this works, let's stay with our paper on women pilots in World War II. If you remember, the "A" topic on our general outline was: "Why civilian women pilots entered the war."

Write Papers

When we took notes, we assigned the following headlines to various "A" note cards: "Women pilot proposal," "Shortage of male pilots," and "Test program approved."

If we decided to use chronological order for our paper, we would shuffle our "A" note cards accordingly—cards marked "Shortage of male pilots" would go first, because the shortage was happened first. All cards marked "Women pilot proposal" come next, followed by cards marked "Test program begun."

Add any miscellaneous cards

After you sort all the cards that have been assigned a specific topic heading, review cards that are still marked with an asterisk. Try to fit them in your stack of cards.

Don't force a note card in. If there doesn't seem to be any logical place for the information on the card, it may be that the data just isn't relevant to your thesis. Set the card aside in a "leftover" pile. You can try again later.

Your detailed outline is done!

Flip through your note cards from front to back. See that? You've created a detailed outline without even knowing it. The topic letters on your note cards match the main topics of your outline. And those headlines on your note cards? They're the subtopics for your outline.

For example, the first part of our detailed outline for our "women pilots" paper would be:

    A. Why civilian women pilots entered the war effort
       1. Shortage of male pilots
       2. Women pilot proposal
       3. Test program begun

We simply transferred our note-card headlines to paper—they appear on our outline in the same order as they appear in our stack of cards.

Some instructors like to approve your outline before letting you proceed with your paper. If yours does, find out the specific outline format you are to follow. You may need to use a different numbering/lettering format from the one shown above—Roman numerals instead of capital letters for topic headings, for example.

Otherwise, you can get as detailed as you like with your outline. In most cases, a two-level outline—with topic headings plus subheadings—will do. Remember that you must have at least two entries at every outline level.

Here's an example of a detailed outline for our "women pilots" paper, which presumes that we decided to organize our paper in chronological order:

Sample Detailed Outline

The Women's Air Force Service in World War II

A. Why civilian women pilots entered the war effort
1. Shortage of male pilots
2. Women pilot proposal
3. Test program begun
B. The type and number of women who participated
1. Statistics on number of initial participants
2. Background information about leaders of the program

      3. Participants' socio-economic background

C. Their qualifications and training
      1. Experience needed to be accepted into the program
      2. Training program
         a. ground school
         b. flight school
         c. exams

D. Their missions and contributions
      1. Ferrying planes
      2. Towing targets
      3. Testing repaired planes
      4. Success vs. male pilots

E. The military vs. civilian status question
      1. Reason for initial civilian status
      2. Plan to militarize
      3. Why plan was needed
      4. Why plan was not carried out

F. The disbanding of the group
      1. Additional pilots no longer needed
      2. Male pilots wanted jobs taken over by women
      3. Support for/against disbanding

G. The fight to be recognized as veterans
      1. Importance of the fight
         a. veterans' benefits for the women
         b. recognition of the group's contributions
      2. Instrumental women in the fight
      3. Debate and vote in Congress
      4. Outcome and effect of vote

By George, I think you've got it!

If you haven't figured it out before, you should understand now why this note-card system is so valuable. If you had written all of your notes on several dozen sheets of paper, it would be quite a task to sort out information and put it in some logical order, let alone reorder it at will.

And this isn't the only stage at which having your notes on individual cards comes in handy. As you'll see in Chapter 7, the note-card system also is helpful when you tackle the next phase of your paper: writing your rough draft.

Chapter Seven

WRITING YOUR ROUGH DRAFT

For some reason, this step is the hardest for most people. It's psychological, I guess—a fear that when your thoughts actually appear in black and white, there for all the world to read, you'll be judged a complete fool.

Well, you can't do a research paper without writing. And since the job has to be done, you might as well face it right now.

Using this book, you'll find this step a lot easier than your friends probably will. Assuming, of course, that you've done everything as instructed so far—taken good notes, organized your note cards and prepared a detailed outline.

You may not have realized it, but you've already *done* a lot of the hard work that goes into the writing stage. You have thought about how your paper will flow. You have organized your notes. And you have prepared a detailed outline. All that's left is to transfer your information and ideas from note cards to paper.

Still, as a writer, I know that this can be a scary prospect, no matter how well you've done up to now . So, in this chapter, I'll show you some tips and tricks that will make writing your rough draft a bit easier.

Because the things you will learn in this chapter and Chapter 8 work together, read both chapters before you begin to write. Then come back and actually work through the steps outlined here.

Set the stage for good writing

Unfortunately for the party-lovers of this world, writing is a solitary activity. Good writing takes concentration and thought. And concentration and thought require quiet—and lots of it!

Find a quiet place to work, and do what you can to make sure you won't be interrupted. Nothing's more maddening than having the perfect phrase on the tip of your brain, only to have a friend pop in and wipe it out of your mind forever.

(As I continually point out in all these books, there are very few hard-and-fast study rules. And this is *not* one of them. Just as some of you may find it very easy to study with the radio blaring, a few of you may not need all this quiet to write, and write well. In fact, too much quiet may work against you. Do what works for *you*. As I've mentioned before, I tend to write, study and do a lot of other "concentration-required" tasks with the radio pounding away. I even took notes and organized my first book while watching daytime television—though writing anything of worth while watching TV can't, I'm convinced, be accomplished.)

You also need to have plenty of desk space, so you can spread out your note cards. Your work area should be well-lit. And you should have a dictionary and thesaurus close at hand. (And if you need even more help than this brief synopsis, get a copy of another book in my **HOW TO STUDY** *Program—Manage Your Time*—where all of this is discussed in far more detail.)

If possible, work on a computer, so that you can add, delete and rearrange your words easily. Don't worry if your computer software doesn't have all the latest bells and whistles—a simple word-processing program is all you really need.

Don't psych yourself out

If you go into this thinking you're going to turn out a teacher-ready paper on your first try, you're doomed. That kind of performance pressure leads only to anxiety and frustration.

At this point, your goal is to produce a rough draft—with the emphasis on *rough*. Your first draft isn't *supposed* to be perfect. It's *supposed* to need revision.

Relax your expectations, and you'll find that your ideas will flow much more freely. You'll be surprised at the intelligent, creative thoughts that come out of that brain of yours when you're not so worried about making a mistake.

Build the foundation first

The essence of good writing has little to do with grammar, spelling, punctuation and the like. The essence of good writing is good thinking.

Sure, the mechanics of writing are important. And you do need to make sure that you have everything spelled just right, that your participles aren't dangling, your periods and commas are placed just so.

But your thoughts, ideas and logic are the foundation of your paper. And you need to build a foundation before you worry about hanging the front door. So, for now, just concentrate on getting your thoughts on paper. Don't worry about using exactly the "right" word. Don't worry about getting commas in all the right places. We'll take care of all that polishing later.

Do a note card draft

Your note cards helped you come up with a detailed outline. Now, they're going to serve you again—helping you plot out the paragraphs and sentences of your paper.

We're going to do some more sorting and rearranging of cards. The end result will be what I call a "note-card draft." Here's what you do:

1. Your note cards should be arranged in the same order as your detailed outline. Take out all of the note cards labeled with the letter of the first topic on your outline.
2. Out of that stack, take out all the cards marked with the same "headline" as the first subheading in your outline.
3. Look at the information on those cards, and think about how the various statistics, quotes and facts might fit together in a paragraph.
4. Rearrange those cards so they fall in the order you have determined is best for the paragraph.
5. Do this for each group of cards, until you reach the end of the deck.

Write Papers

To illustrate this process, let's use the example of our paper on women pilots.

Suppose we have 25 note cards with information related to the first topic heading in our outline—"Why civilian women pilots entered the war." And suppose that four of those 25 cards have information related to the first subtopic—"Shortage of male pilots."

Here's the information on each card:

Card #1:   Quote from a general about the seriousness of the pilot shortage

Card #2:   Statistics about how many pilots were needed and the number available for active duty

Card #3:   Brief explanation of why there was a shortage

Card #4:   Description of the type of jobs that weren't getting done because of the pilot shortage

How could we string these four pieces of information together into a paragraph or series of paragraphs? Here's one solution:

1. Start out with the statistic (card 2)
2. Explain reasons for the shortage (card 3)
3. Discuss the kind of jobs that needed to be filled (card 4)
4. Wrap up with the general's quote, which serves to summarize and emphasize the key point of the section (card 1)

This decided, we simply shuffle the note cards so that they fall in that order. Then we move on through the rest of our note cards, continuing to create new paragraphs, until our entire paper is mapped out.

Building good paragraphs

I don't want to get into a lengthy discussion of English composition here, but since we're dealing with how to build the paragraphs in your paper, it makes sense to stop for a brief discussion of what's involved in good paragraph construction.

Each paragraph in your paper is like a mini-essay. It should have a topic sentence—a statement of the key point or fact you will discuss in the paragraph—and contain the evidence to support it. You shouldn't expect your reader to believe that your topic sentence is true just because you say so—you must back up your point with hard data. This evidence can come in different forms, such as:

- Quotes from experts
- Research statistics
- Examples from research or from your own experience
- Detailed descriptions or other background information

Paragraphs are like bricks of information—stack them up, one by one, until you have built a wall of evidence. Construct each paragraph carefully, and your readers will have no choice but to agree with your final conclusion.

If paragraphs are the bricks in your wall of evidence, transitions—a sentence or phrase that moves the reader from one thought to another—are the mortar that holds them together. Smooth transitions help readers move effortlessly from the summary of one paragraph to the introduction of another. (The first sentence in the paragraph you have just read is an example of a transition.)

Now put it all on paper

It's time to take the plunge and turn your note card draft into a written rough draft. Using your cards as your guide, sit down and write.

Double- or triple-space your draft—that will make it easier to edit later. After you are finished with each note card, put a check mark at the bottom.

If you decide that you won't include information from a particular card, don't throw the card away—yet. Keep it in a separate stack. You may decide to fit in that piece of information in another part of your paper. Or change your mind after you read your rough draft and decide to include the information where you had originally planned.

If you get stuck...

Got writer's block already? Here are a few tricks to get you unstuck:

- *Pretend you're writing to a good friend*—just tell him or her everything you've learned about your subject and why you believe your thesis is correct.
- *Use everyday language.* Too many people get so hung up on using fancy words and phrases that they forget that their goal is to *communicate.* Simpler is better.
- *Just do it.* What is it about a blank computer screen or piece of paper that scares would-be writers so badly? It happens to almost everyone, and there's only one cure I know: Just type *some*thing...*any*thing. Once you have written that first paragraph—even if it's a really *bad* first paragraph—your brain will start to generate spontaneous ideas.

- *Don't edit yourself!* As you write your rough draft, don't keep beating yourself up with negative thoughts such as "This sounds really stupid" or "I'm a terrible writer. Why can't I express that better?" Remember: Your goal is a *rough* draft—it's supposed to stink a bit.

- *Keep moving.* If you get hung up in a particular section, don't sit there stewing over it for hours—or even for many minutes. Just write a quick note about what you plan to cover in that section, then go on to the next section.

  For example: "Talk about how women pilots were ridiculed by men in the air forces at first. Mention instances quoted from resource #12. Add statistics that proved women could do the job."

- *If you can't get even that much out,* skip the section altogether and come back to it later. The point is, *do whatever you have to do to keep moving forward.* Force yourself to make it all the way through your paper, with as few stops as possible.

The trouble with plagiarism

It's so tempting. You're having trouble with a sentence or section. The information you need was explained beautifully in that article you found in an old magazine. Why not just copy the section from the article? It so musty and obscure your teacher couldn't possibly know what you've done. Why not do it?

Because that would be plagiarism, that's why. And plagiarism—passing off another person's words or ideas as your own—is the biggest no-no of research-paper writing. It's a sure way to bring your grade down, down, down. It may even get you a failing mark. And, grades aside, it is simply *wrong*.

"But who'll ever know that I didn't write it myself?" you wonder. Sorry, but the odds are about 999 to 1 that you *will* be found out.

First, your teacher probably has been reading research papers—some of them undoubtedly on the same subject as yours—for a good many years. Those same "perfect passages" tend to pop up again and again. Do you really think your teacher will believe it's a coincidence that you wrote the exact same paragraph as that student in *last* year's class? Who flunked, by the way.

Second, your teacher is familiar with your work and your writing style. That "borrowed" paragraph, written in someone else's style, is going to be noticeably different from your own deathless prose.

Then, of course, there is the moral issue involved—but I won't get into that. You learned that stealing was wrong in kindergarten. The principle applies to written words and ideas, too.

And how to avoid it

To avoid plagiarism, you must give proper credit to the original author of material you use. You must also give credit for any facts, figures or research data that you use. You do this through a *source note*—a footnote, endnote or parenthetical note.

Sometimes, you might want to include a sentence or entire paragraph exactly as it was written by another author. If you do this, you must enclose the material in quotation marks and copy the material word for word, comma for comma. And you must offset the paragraph from the rest of the paper by indenting it from both margins, like this:

> "The author's paragraph you're quoting word for word is set off from the rest of the section by indenting it from both margins. It also is enclosed in quotation marks."

You should use this device sparingly, and only if the segment is so eloquently written or so meaningful that it makes a special impact on the reader.

You should *not* do this to fill up your paper "the easy way"—if your teacher is anything like most of mine were, he won't buy seven pages of quotes in a 10-page paper.

We'll talk about how to write source notes in the next chapter. Because it's easiest to note which statements or sentences need documenting as you prepare your rough draft, go ahead and read Chapter 8 now.

But that's your only excuse for stopping or delaying your writing! As soon as you've learned the specifics about source notes, sit right down and finish your rough draft. If you keep in mind everything we've talked about in this chapter, writing your draft will be easier than you think.

I promise!

Chapter Eight

DOCUMENTING YOUR SOURCES

You must give credit to the source of any facts, expressions or ideas you use in your paper that are not your own. In this chapter, you'll learn the specifics of how to do that.

For many years, the preferred way to credit (or *document*) sources was the *footnote*. Two other forms of documentation—*endnotes* and *parenthetical notes*—are popular now as well. For convenience, I'll refer to all of these different forms collectively as "source notes."

Whose rules are they, anyway?

In an earlier chapter, we discussed the fact that different authorities have set out different rules for bibliography listings.

The same is true for source notes. Ask your instructor whose rules you are to follow.

If your teacher doesn't have a preference, you can use the method that seems easiest to you. But use the same method consistently throughout your paper—don't use a footnote on one page, an endnote on another.

Again, I'm going to give you the Modern Language Association of America (MLA) rules. And again, I'll give you the rules for three basic types of materials: a book, magazine article and newspaper article. You can consult the *MLA Handbook* or other reference book if you want specific examples of how to prepare notes for more complicated types of material.

A reminder: What needs documentation

You need a source note when you put any of the following in your paper:

- Quotations taken from a published source
- Someone else's theories or ideas
- Someone else's sentences, phrases or special expressions
- Facts, figures and research data compiled by someone else
- Graphs, pictures and charts designed by someone else

There are some exceptions: You don't need to document the source of a fact, theory or expression that is common knowledge. And you don't need a source note when you use a phrase or expression for which there is no known author.

For example, if you mention that Paris is the capital of France, you don't need to document the source of that information. Ditto for time-worn phrases as "When in Rome, do as the Romans do" or "a stitch in time, saves nine."

For a test of whether a statement needs a source note, ask yourself whether readers would otherwise think that you had come up with the information or idea all by yourself. If the answer is "yes," you need a source note. If you're in doubt, include a source note anyway.

Footnotes

A footnote is a source note that appears at the "foot" (bottom) of a page of text. The footnote system works like this: You put a raised (superscript) number at the end of the statement or fact you need to document. This serves as a "flag" to readers—it tells them to look at the bottom of the page for a note about the source of the data.

In front of that footnote, you put the same superscript number as you put next to the statement or fact in your text. This tells the reader which footnote applies to which statement or fact of text.

There is no limit to the number of footnotes you may have in your paper. Number each footnote consecutively, starting with the number 1. For every footnote "flag" in your paper, be sure there is a corresponding source note at the bottom of the page.

What goes into a footnote

You put the same information in your footnote as you do in your bibliography listing, with two differences: In a footnote, the author's name is shown in normal order, and the exact page number on which the information being documented appeared in the source is cited.

Most of the information for your footnotes will come from your bibliography cards. But you'll have to look at your note cards to get the actual page number from which various facts came. Arrange elements as follows:

1. Name of the author(s), first name first
2. Title of the book or article
3. Publication information—place of publication, name of the publisher, date of publication, etc.
4. The number of the page(s) on which the information appeared in the work

As with bibliography listings, the content of a footnote depends on the type of reference material. For a refresher on the specific information that you need to include and in what order, see the lists in Chapter 10.

Typing your footnotes

The following general rules apply to all footnotes:

- Put footnotes four lines below the last line of text on the page.
- Indent the first line of a footnote five spaces.
- Single-space lines within an individual footnote; double-space between footnotes.
- Always put the superscript (raised) number of the footnote after the punctuation in your text.
- Abbreviate all months except May, June and July.

Punctuation guidelines for footnotes

There are specific rules of punctuation and style to follow when you write your footnotes.

For a book, type:

1. The number of the note (superscript)
2. Author's first name, middle name or initial (if any), last name (comma)
3. Title of the book (underlined). No period after the title
4. In parentheses—the place of publication (colon); name of the publisher (comma); year of publication
5. The exact page(s) on which the information you're documenting appears (period). Do not write "page" or "pg." or "p."—just the number

For a magazine article, type:

1. The number of the note (superscript)
2. Author's first name, middle name or initial (if any), last name (comma)
3. In quotation marks—title of the article (comma)
4. Name of the periodical in which the article appeared (underlined)
5. The day the periodical was published (for a weekly or biweekly periodical); the month; the year (colon)
6. The exact page number(s) from which the information was taken (period)

For a newspaper article, type:

1. The number of the note (superscript)
2. Author's first name, middle name or initial (if any), last name (comma)
3. In quotation marks—title of the article (comma)
4. Name of the newspaper in which the article appeared (underlined)
5. Name of the city and town in which the paper is published (if not part of the name of the paper and/or if the paper is not widely known)—enclose in brackets and do *not* underline
6. The day the paper was published; the month; the year (comma)
7. The edition (abbreviate "edition" as "ed.") if there is more than one published per day (colon)
8. The section and exact page from which the information was taken (period)

Remember, if there is other information on your bibliography card—e.g., the name of an editor or series—you need to include it in your footnote. Arrange information in the same order as you would for a bibliography listing. (See chapter 10 for the correct order.)

Second references

The second time you cite a particular reference as a source of information, you use an abbreviated form of the footnote—just the author's last name and the page number on which the information appeared. (See sample footnote #4 following.)

If you have taken information from two different books written by the same author, you need to include the title of the book as well.

If there is no author given for the work, show the title plus the page number.

Sample footnotes

Below is a sample excerpt from a research paper, followed by four sample footnotes—three to show the different styles necessary for various sources (book, magazine article and news-paper article), the fourth to illustrate how to cite a source for the second time:

> Bob Smith was a leader in the history of Smiths in America. He earned $1 million by the time he was 18.[1] He was awarded honorary degrees in law from Harvard and Princeton.[2] At the age of 35, he invented the first successful widget-spinning gadget,[3] which gave manufacturers a new way to produce widgets.
>
> More than a savvy businessman and accomplished scholar, Smith was a devoted family man. A close friend and neighbor, Bill Jones, once said of Smith: "I never met a man who spent so much time attending to the needs of his wife and children."[4]

[1] Karen A. Jones, The Life and Times of Bob Smith (New York: Smith Press, 1989) 24.

[2] Stan Perkins, "The Life and Times of Bob Smith," Smith Magazine 24 Apr. 1989: 22.

3 Bill Black, "Bob Smith: The New Widget Spinner," The New York Times 16 June 1976, late ed.: A12.

4 Jones 38.

Endnotes

Endnotes are basically the same thing as footnotes. Within the body of your paper, you indicate the existence of an endnote in the same manner as for footnotes—with a superscript (raised) number. The only difference is that you put all of the source listings together—on a separate page at the end of the text—instead of at the bottom of each page.

Title the last page of your paper "Notes" and center that title at the top of the page. Leave a one-inch margin on all sides of the paper (top, bottom, left and right).

List endnotes consecutively (put endnote 1 first, then note 2, etc.). As with your footnotes, indent the first line of each note. Double-space the entire page (both within individual notes and between notes). Follow the same punctuation rules as those given for footnotes.

Parenthetical notes

Parenthetical notes are probably the easiest way to document sources.

In this system, you put a brief source note right in the body of your text, enclosed in parentheses (hence, the name—parenthetical notes).

Generally, your reference includes only the last name of the author and the page number from which the information was taken. For example:

> Bob Smith was a leader in the history of Smiths in America. He earned a million dollars by the time he was 18 (Jones 24).

To find complete details about the source, readers refer to your bibliography. In this case, they would look for a book or article by "(Somebody) Jones."

Make sure your note includes enough information so your readers will know exactly which source in your bibliography you are citing.

For example, if your bibliography lists two different works, both written by authors with the last name of Jones., you should include the author's first name in your parenthetical note—i.e., (Karen Jones 24.)

If you have two books written by the same author, include the title of the book you are citing. You can use a one- or two-word abbreviation of the title, if you want.: (Jones, Life and Times 24.)

If your source is a one-page article, you don't have to give any page number in your note.

Now or later?

You can incorporate your source notes as you write your rough draft, or you can put them in during a later draft. I suggest you do the following:

1. As you write your rough draft, mark any statement of fact that needs to be documented. Note the number of the source (the number in the upper left-hand corner of your note card) and the page number from which the material was taken. For example: "Bob

Smith was awarded honorary degrees from Harvard and Princeton. (#2-22)."

2. As you prepare your final draft, simply convert these "preliminary" notes into your formal ones.

3. Continue on through the rest of your text, consecutively numbering each note.

4. *If you are using footnotes or endnotes:* When you come to the first "preliminary" note in your text, replace the letter and number code with the superscript numeral "1." Find the bibliography card with the same source number as that in your preliminary note. Type your footnote or endnote, using the data from the bibliography card. Use the same page number that you show in your "preliminary" note.

5. *If you are using parenthetical notes:* Find the bibliography card that matches the source number in your preliminary note. Replace the number-letter code with your parenthetical note. Again, you already know which page number to cite, since you had that information in your preliminary note.

(Of course, if you're working on a computer, this will only work if you print out a hard copy of your rough draft. When you replace your "preliminary" note letter-number code, you'll lose the information about which source and page number you need to cite.)

Take a deep breath. We're almost there!

Chapter Nine

REVISING YOUR MASTERPIECE

You can breathe a big sigh of relief—your rough draft is done!

Now, you need to take that rough-cut diamond and polish it into a sparkling gem.

In the remaining chapters of this book, we'll revise your rough cut—and revise it again—until we arrive at your final draft.

As we've done with other parts of your assignment, we'll break this process into several steps.

In this chapter, we'll work through two of those steps.

First, you'll edit your paper for content and clarity.

Then, we'll work on the finer points—grammar, spelling, sentence construction, etc.

Phase 1: Edit for meaning

As I said, we're not going to handle all your revisions in one pass. At this point, you still don't need to concentrate on grammar, spelling and other technical aspects of your paper. Of course, when you notice flaws in these areas, fix them. But don't get hung up on them right now.

Rather, during *this* phase of the revision process, you should be trying to:

- *Improve* the flow of your paper—from paragraph to paragraph, sentence to sentence;
- *Organize* your thoughts and information better;
- *Clarify* any confusing points;
- *Strengthen* any weak arguments—by explaining your argument better or adding more data to support your point of view.

Revision checklist

As you review your rough draft, ask yourself the following questions:

- Do your thoughts move logically from one point to the next?
- Is the meaning of every sentence and paragraph crystal clear?
- Does every sentence make a point—or support one?
- Do you move smoothly from one paragraph to the next? Or do you jump randomly from one topic to another?

Write Papers

- Do you support your conclusions with solid evidence—research data, examples, statistics?

- Do you include a good *mix* of evidence—quotes from experts, scientific data, personal experiences, historical examples?

- Do you have a solid introduction and conclusion?

- Did you write in your own words and style? Or have you merely strung together phrases and quotes "borrowed" from other authors?

- Have you explained your subject thoroughly? Or assumed that readers have more knowledge about it than they actually might? (Remember: *You're* familiar with the topic now, but you've spent *weeks* on it. Just because something is now "obvious" to you doesn't mean your readers will know what you're talking about.)

- Have you convinced your readers that your thesis is valid?

Mark any trouble spots with a colored pencil or pen. If you have an idea of how to fix a section, jot it down on your rough draft.

Then, ask a friend or parent to read your paper. Ask them which sections were confusing, which didn't seem to fit in as written. Make notes on your draft about these trouble points.

Now, sit down and begin to rewrite. Focus on all of those problem areas you found. If necessary, add new information. Play with sentences, paragraphs, even entire sections.

If you're working with a computer, this is fairly easy to do. You can flip words, cut and add sentences, rearrange whole pages with a few keystrokes.

If you're still hunched over a typewriter or scratching along with pen and paper, you can do the same thing, using scissors and tape. Just cut up the pages of your rough draft and tape them together in their new order.

If you can't figure out how to fix a bothersome sentence or paragraph, take a time-out from writing. Think about what it is you're trying to tell the reader—what point are you trying to get across?

Once you get your thoughts straight, the words will usually take care of themselves.

Phase 2: Do the detail work

When you finish editing for content and meaning, print or type out a clean copy of your paper.

It's time to double-check all of your facts for accuracy. And deal with those things I've been telling you to delay: sentence structure, grammar, punctuation, spelling, etc.

Comb through your paper, and check every piece of factual information against your note cards:

- Did you spell names, terms and places correctly?

- When you quoted dates and statistics, did you get your numbers straight?

- Do you have a source note (or preliminary source note) for every fact, expression or idea that is not your own?

- If you quoted material from a source, did you quote that source exactly, word for word, comma for comma? And did you put the material in quotation marks?

Mark any corrections on your new draft. Again, use a colored pen or pencil so you'll easily spot corrections later.

Smooth out the edges

You've already fixed major problem areas in your paper. Now take an even closer look at your sentences and paragraphs. Try to make them smoother, tighter, easier to understand.

- Is there too much fat? Seize every opportunity to make the same point in fewer words.

- Are there places where phrasing or construction is awkward? Try to rearrange the sentence or section so that it has a better flow.

- Did you use descriptive, colorful words? Did you tell your reader "The planes were damaged" or paint a more colorful and creative picture: "The planes were broken-down hulks of rusted metal—bullet-ridden, neglected warbirds that could barely limp down the runway."

- Consult your thesaurus for synonyms that might do a better job than the words you originally chose. But don't get carried away and use words so obscure that the average reader wouldn't know their meaning. When in doubt, opt for the familiar word rather than the obscure, the shorter vs. the longer, the tangible vs. the hypothetical, the direct word vs. the roundabout phrase.

- Have you overused particular words? Constantly relying on the same verb or adjective makes your writing boring. Again, check your thesaurus for other possibilities.

- How do the words *sound?* When you read your paper aloud, does it flow like a rhythmic piece of music? Or plod along like a dirge? Vary the length of your sentences and paragraphs to make your writing more exciting.

- Always remember the point of the paper—to communicate your ideas as clearly and concisely as possible. So don't get lost in the details. Yes, we've all heard of one famous writer or another (Flaubert comes immediately to mind) who filled a wastebasket with discarded pages before he got one page of usable prose. Whose every word seems to be drawn screaming and kicking from her belly. Hey, this isn't *War and Peace* you're writing here. Relax. If you have to choose between that "perfect" word and the most organized paper imaginable, opt for the latter.

Again, mark corrections on your draft with a colored pen or pencil. No need to retype your paper yet—unless it's gotten so marked up that it's hard to read!

Check your grammar and spelling

All right, here's the part that almost nobody enjoys. It's time to rid your paper of mistakes in grammar and spelling.

I know that I've told you all along that your thoughts are the most important element of your paper. It's true. But it's also true that glaring mistakes in grammar and spelling will lead your teacher to believe that you are either careless or downright ignorant. Neither of which will bode well for your final grade.

So, get out your dictionary and a reference book on English usage and grammar. If you don't happen to own the latter, check one out from the library, or better yet, buy your own copy. Ask your instructor to recommend a few good choices.

Write Papers

Scour through your paper, sentence by sentence, marking corrections with your colored pen or pencil. Ferret out:

- **Misspelled words.** Check every word. Ask yourself: "If I had to bet $100 that I spelled that word correctly, would I pull out my wallet?" No? Then you'd better look it up in the dictionary! Watch out especially for the words your spell-check program may not catch, like "too" instead of "to."

- **Incorrect punctuation.** Review the rules regarding placement of commas, quotation marks, periods, etc. Make sure you follow those rules throughout your paper.

- **Incorrect sentence structure.** Look for dangling participles, split infinitives, sentences that end in prepositions and other "no-no's." Again, review the rules about such matters in your reference book.

Phase 3: Prepare the almost-final draft

Retype your paper, making all those corrections you marked as you completed Phase 2. As you prepare this draft of your paper, incorporate the following three steps:

1. Format the paper according to your teacher's instructions—use the specified page length, margins and line spacing. If you haven't been given any instructions in this area, follow these guidelines:
   - Type or print on one side of the paper only.
   - Use 8 1/2" x 11" paper.
   - Leave a one-inch margin all around—top, bottom, right and left.

- Indent the first word of each paragraph five spaces from the left margin.
- Double-space all text. (Single-space footnotes, but double space between each.)
- Number your pages in the upper right-hand corner of the paper, one half-inch from the top.

Think this is an inconsequential step? Don't kid yourself. After all, if you can't follow the simplest directions about things like margins, why should your instructor believe that you've gotten anything else correct?

2. Incorporate your final footnotes, endnotes or parenthetical notes. For specifics on how to do this, refer back to Chapter 8.

3. Give your paper a title, if you haven't already done so. Your title should be as short and sweet as possible, but it should tell readers what they can expect to learn from your paper. Don't get cute or coy—that's for magazine covers (and it's pretty annoying even then).

You may want to have a headline and a subhead—for example, "Women Air Force Service Pilots: The Almost-forgotten Veterans of World War II." If so, separate your subhead from your main head with a colon and two spaces.

Some teachers prefer that you put your title, name, date and class number on a separate title page. Others want this information to appear at the top of the first page of your text. As always, ask your instructor which page format to follow.

Now, give yourself a big pat on the back! The toughest parts of your assignment are all behind you now.

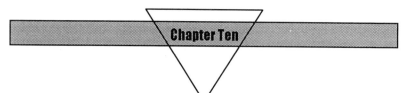

Chapter Ten

COMPILING YOUR FINAL BIBLIOGRAPHY

By the time you've completed the revision process outlined in Chapter 9, your paper should be in very good shape. Give yourself a round of applause!

There's just a little bit left to do now. You need to prepare your final bibliography, which I'll show you how to do in this chapter. Lastly, you'll need to proofread your paper and type your final draft. Those steps are covered in Chapter 11.

"Works consulted" vs. "works cited"

Your teacher may ask you to do a *"works consulted"* bibliography—a list of all reference materials you reviewed during your research, *even if nothing from them was incorporated in your paper.* Or, you may be asked to do a *"works cited"* bibliography—listing only those materials you mentioned in your footnotes, endnotes or parenthetical notes.

If your teacher does not specify which type of bibliography to include, choose the first. It will be a better indication of the range of research you've done.

There are some very specific technical rules you must follow when preparing your bibliography. These rules are the same whether you are doing a "works consulted" or "works cited" bibliography.

Your bibliography listings contain virtually the same information as a footnote or endnote. But as we've already learned, there are two big variations: 1) The format and punctuation are different, and 2) the page number references are different.

No, I don't know why. Somewhere along the line, people made up these rules. I'm sure there were good reasons for the things they decided. But the reasons behind the rules aren't important. What *is* important is that you follow the rules—like them or not.

Remember, different authorities prefer different rules, so check with your teacher to find out which rules he or she prefers you follow. Because we've been following MLA rules so far, we'll stick with them.

Laying out your bibliography page

Your bibliography should be at the end of your paper, on a separate page or pages:

- One inch from the top of the each page: Center the title "Works Cited" or "Works Consulted," depending upon which type of bibliography you are doing.
- Use the same margins as you did for the rest of your paper—one inch all the way around.

- Treat your bibliography pages as if they are a continuation of the text of your paper and number them accordingly—*don't* start repaginating.

- List materials in alphabetical order, by the author's last name. If no author is given, go by the first word in the title of the work (unless the first word is "A," "An" or "The," in which case go by the second word).

- The first line of each listing should be flush with the left margin. Indent all lines *except* the first five spaces from the left margin.

- Double-space all listings. And double-space between entries.

- Abbreviate all months except May, June and July.

Sort out your bibliography cards

You will take all the information for your bibliography from your bibliography cards. Before you begin typing, put your bibliography cards in the correct alphabetical order. Then, just transfer information, card by card, following the style guidelines listed below.

For a bibliography listing for a book, type:

1. The author's last name (comma), first name and middle name or initial (period and skip two spaces)

2. The title of the book, underlined (period and skip two spaces)

3. The place of publication (colon and skip a space), the name of the publisher (comma, skip a space), the year of publication (period)

For a magazine article, type:

1. The author's last name (comma), first name and middle name or initial (period and skip two spaces)
2. The title of the article (in quotation marks, with a period before the ending quotation marks, then skip two spaces). Note: If the name of the article ends with its own punctuation, such as a question mark, don't put in the period
3. The title of the periodical in which the article appeared, underlined
4. The day of publication (if one is given); the month; the year; (colon and space)
5. The page numbers on which the article appeared (period). If the article didn't appear on consecutive pages, follow the first page by a plus (+) sign—e.g., 23+

You do not need to include the volume numbers of a magazine, unless it is a scholarly journal. But if in doubt, include it—better too much information than too little.

For a newspaper article, type:

1. The author's last name (comma), first name and middle name or initial (period and skip two spaces)
2. The title of the article (in quotation marks, with a period before the ending quotation marks, then skip two spaces). Note: If the name of the article ends with its own punctuation, such as a question mark, don't put in the period
3. The title of the newspaper in which the article appeared, underlined
4. The day of publication; the month; the year

5. *If the paper publishes more than one daily edition:* Put a comma after the year, then type the edition information (colon and a space), then the page numbers on which the article appeared. Include the section letter or number if applicable—e.g., A8, etc.

6. *If the paper publishes only one daily edition:* Type a *colon* after the year (space), then the section and page numbers on which the article appeared

If the newspaper isn't a nationally published or well-known paper, add the name of the city and state where it is published after the title. Enclose this information in brackets, but don't underline it. Example: Lawrence Times [Lawrence, NJ]

You do not need to include the volume or issue numbers of the newspaper.

Sample bibliography listings

This excerpt from a sample bibliography page includes listings for a book, a magazine article and a magazine article (in that order):

Jones, Karen A. <u>The Life and Times of Bob Smith.</u> New York: Smith Press, 1989.

Perkins, Stan. "The Life and Times of Bob Smith." <u>Smith Magazine</u> 24 Apr. 1989: 22-28.

Black, Bill. "Bob Smith: The New Widget Spinner." <u>New York Times</u> 16 June 1976, late ed.: A12.

Did you get them all?

Check your bibliography against the text of your paper. Be sure that you have included all the works cited in your source notes.

Chapter Eleven

APPLYING THE FINISHING TOUCHES

Can you see it? That light at the end of the tunnel? You should—you're 99 percent of the way *through* the research-paper tunnel.

Don't shut down your mental engine just yet, though—there are a couple of tricky turns left to negotiate.

First, you need to proofread your paper. Then, you need to type or print out a perfect copy of your manuscript—and proofread it again.

To be a good proofreader, you need a sharp eye. Unfortunately, your poor eyes are probably pretty tired by now. And you've become so familiar with your paper that it may be difficult for you to see it clearly. You're likely to read phrase by phrase, rather than word by word. And that means that you'll likely skip right over some typos and other errors.

Not to worry, though. In this chapter, I'll show you some tricks that will help you overcome these problems and catch all those little bugaboos in your manuscript.

Trick # 1: Read your paper aloud

Go to a quiet room, and read your paper aloud. Not in your head—actually speak the words you have written. Sound them out, syllable by syllable. You'll quickly pick up on typos and misspelled words.

Mark any errors that you find with a brightly colored pen or pencil, and circle them. You want to be able to spot them easily and quickly when you type up your final draft.

Trick #2: Work backward

This is another great trick. Read your paper from back to front, starting with the last word on the last page, working backward toward your introduction. This will help you to focus on each individual word, rather than on the meaning of your phrases and sentences.

Trick #3: Use your computer "spell check"

If you're working on a computer that has a "spell-check" program, be sure to use it. But don't rely on it alone! Yes, the computer will pick up misspelled words. But what if you've used the *wrong* word altogether—used "their" when you meant "there?" If you've *spelled* it right, the computer won't pick up your error. (Some grammar/usage programs will—lucky you if you have one!)

Trick #4: Have someone else read your paper

Ask a parent, sibling, child or other relative to read your paper. Or trade papers with a classmate—you read his if he reads yours. Someone who has never seen your paper before is much more likely to catch a mistake than someone who has read it again and again. (Just be careful about the person you pick and the instructions you give. If you're two days away from turning in your paper, you don't want to hear from your anal-retentive friend how *he* would have organized the paper.)

Prepare your perfect copy

After you've proofread your paper several times *(at least* three times), type or print out a clean draft. Then proofread it *again,* to make sure you caught every single error. Miss one or two? Type up those pages again, *and proofread again.* Continue until you're sure your paper is error-free.

Get it all together

Be sure to put your final draft on good quality, white typing or computer printer paper. Don't use that erasable typing paper! It smudges easily.

If you've written your paper on a computer, avoid printing your final draft on a low-quality, dot matrix or bubble-jet printer. Manuscripts printed on such printers are sometimes hard to read—and the last thing you want to do is make it difficult for your teacher to read your paper. (Some instructors do not even accept such printer copy.)

You can also save your paper on a floppy disk, and take the disk to a quick-print shop. Providing you're working on a compatible computer system, the shop can print out your paper on a laser printer, which produces typeset-quality printing.

If you don't have access to a good printer, or if you're just a lousy typist, you may want to have your final draft prepared by a professional typist or computer service bureau. Just make sure the one you select can have your paper done in plenty of time to meet your final deadline!

As soon as you complete your final draft, head right for the copy shop. Pay the buck or two it costs to make a copy of your paper. In the event that you lose or damage your original manuscript, you will have a backup copy.

Turn in your assignment

Put your paper in a new manuscript binder or folder, unless your instructor asks you to do otherwise. Then, turn in your paper—on time, of course!

And congratulate yourself!

You have just completed one of the most challenging assignments you will face as a student. You should feel a real sense of accomplishment. Remember, you can use many of the same strategies you learned as we put together your research paper when you prepare essays, oral reports and other school assignments (which, as it turns out, I discuss in the next chapter). And the skills you developed during the past few weeks or months will be useful to you long after you've left the classroom behind for good.

So accept my congratulations, and treat yourself to a little celebration.

You took on the dreaded "R" monster.

And you *won!*

Chapter Twelve

ESSAY TESTS AND ORAL REPORTS

Approach essay questions the same way you would a paper. While you can't check your textbook or go to the library to do research, the facts, ideas, comparisons, etc. you need are in your own cerebral library—your mind.

Don't ever, *ever* begin writing the answer to an essay question without a little "homework" first. I don't care if you're the school's prize-winning journalist.

First, really look at the question. Are you sure you know what it's asking? What are the verbs? Don't "describe" when it calls for you to "compare and contrast." Don't "explain" when it tells you to "argue." Underline the verbs. (See pages 112 and 113 for a list of the most-used such verbs in essay tests and what each is instructing you to do.)

Write Papers

Then sit back a minute and think about what you're going to say. Or less than a minute, depending on how much time you have, but *don't* just start writing.

Here's the step-by-step way to answer every essay question:

Step One: On a blank sheet of paper, write down all the facts, ideas, concepts, etc. you feel should be included in your answer.

Step Two: Organize them in the order in which they should appear. You don't have to rewrite your notes into a detailed outline—why not just number each note according to where you want to place it?

Step Three: Compose your first paragraph, working on it just as long and as hard as I suggested you do on your papers. It should summarize and introduce the key points you will make in your essay. *This is where superior essay answers are made or unmade.*

Step Four: Write your essay.

Step Five: Reread your essay and, if necessary, add points left out, correct spelling, grammar, etc. Also watch for a careless omission that could cause serious damage—leaving out a "not", making the point opposite of the one you wanted to.

If there is a particular fact you know is important and should be included but you just don't remember it, guess if you can. Otherwise, just leave it out and do the best you can. If the rest of your essay is well-thought-out and organized and clearly communicates all the other points that should be included, I doubt most teachers will mark you down too severely for such an omission.

Remember: Few teachers will be impressed by length. A well-organized, well-constructed, specific answer to their question will always get you a better grade than "shotgunning"—writing down everything you know in the faint hope that you will actually hit something. Worry less about the specific words and more about the information. Organize your answer to a fault and write to be understood, not to impress. Better to use shorter sentences, paragraphs and words—and be clear and concise—than to let the teacher fall into a clausal nightmare from which he may never emerge (and neither will your "A"!).

If you don't have the faintest clue what the question means, ask. If you still don't have any idea of the answer—and I mean *zilch*—leave it blank. Writing down everything you think you know about the supposed subject in the hopes that one or two things will actually have something to do with the question is, in my mind, a waste of everyone's time. Better to allocate the time you would waste to other parts of the test and do a better job on those.

The best-organized beats the best-written

While I think numbering your notes is as good an organizational tool as jotting down a complete outline, there is certainly nothing wrong with fashioning a quick outline. Not one with Roman numerals—this outline will consist of a simple list of abbreviated words, scribbled on a piece of scrap paper or in the margin of your test booklet. The purpose of this outline is the same as those fancy ones: to make sure you include everything you need and want to say—in order.

No one is going to grade this outline. In fact, no one else is even going to *see* it. I might as well make my "quality, not quantity" speech here, too. I hope you write well. It's important. But excellent writing, even pages and pages of it, will not get you an excellent grade unless you have the quality—hard-hitting, incisive, direct answers.

Again, most teachers won't fall for the beautifully crafted, empty answer. Don't depend on your good looks or your command of the subjunctive to get you by. Go home and study.

Think of the introduction and the conclusion as the bread in a sandwich, with the information in between as the hamburger, lettuce, tomato and pickle. Everything is necessary for it all to hang together, but the main attraction is going to be what's between the slices.

Proof it!

Budget your time so that you can go back over your essay, slowly, and correct any mistakes or make any additions. Check your spelling, punctuation, grammar and syntax. (And if you don't know what that is, find out. You'll need to know for the SAT.) It would be a shame for you to write a beautiful essay and lose points because you had those kinds of errors.

When you're done, you're done...almost

Resist the temptation to leave the room or turn in your paper before you absolutely have to. Imagine the pain of sitting in the cafeteria, while everyone else is back in the room, continuing to work on the test, and you suddenly remember what else you could have said to make your essay really sparkle. But it's too late!

Make sure you can't, simply *can't*, add anything more to any of the essay answers before you walk out of the test.

If you're out of time are you out of luck?

While you should have carefully allocated sufficient time to complete each essay before you started working on the first, things happen. And you may find yourself with two minutes left and one essay to go. What do you do? As quickly as possible, write down everything you think should be included in your answer and number each point in the order in which you would have written it. If you then have time to reorganize your notes into a better-organized outline, do so. Many teachers will give you partial credit (some near *full* credit) if your outline contains all the information the answer was supposed to. It will at least show you knew a lot about the subject and were capable of outlining a response.

One of the reasons you may have left yourself with insufficient time to answer one or more questions is because you knew too darned much about the previous question(s). And you wanted to make sure the teacher *knew* you knew, so you wrote...and wrote...and wrote...until you ran out of time. Be careful—some teachers throw in a relatively general question that, if you wanted to, you could write about until next Wednesday. In that case, they aren't testing your knowledge of the whole subject as much as your ability to *edit* yourself, to organize and summarize the *important* points. Just remember that no matter how fantastic your answer to any one essay, it is going to get 1/5 the overall score (presuming five questions)—that is, 20 points, never more, even if you turn in a publishable book manuscript. Meanwhile, 80 points are waiting for you.

Oral reports

There are some key differences between writing a report and presenting it orally, especially if you don't want to make the mistake of just reading your report in front of the class.

Good notes are your lifeline when you stand up to say what's on your mind. They should act as cues to remind you where your talk should go next, and they should make you feel secure that you can get through the ordeal.

Common Instructional Verbs on Essay Tests

Compare   Examine two or more objects, ideas, people, etc. and note similarities and differences.

Contrast   Compare to highlight differences.

Criticize   Judge and discuss the merits and faults of (similarly, **critique**)

Define   Explain or identify the nature or essential qualities of.

Describe   Convey the appearance, nature, attributes, etc. of something

Discuss   Consider or examine by argument, comment, etc.; debate; explore solutions.

Enumerate   List various events, things, descriptions, ideas, etc.

Evaluate   Appraise the worth of an idea, comment, etc. and justify your conclusion.

Explain   Make the meaning of something clear, plain, intelligible and/or understandable.

Illustrate   Use specific examples or analogies to clarify or explain.

Interpret   Give the meaning of something by paraphrase, by translation or by an explanation based on personal opinion.

Justify   Defend or uphold a statement, decision or conclusion.

Narrate   Similar to **describe**, but only applicable to something that happens in time. Hence, it is to recount the occurrence of something, usually by giving details of events in the order in which they occurred.

Outline   Do a general sketch, account or report, indicating only the main features of a book, subject or project.

Prove   Establish the truth or genuineness of by evidence or argument. (In math, verify validity by mathematical demonstration.)

Relate   Give an account of happenings, events and/or circumstances, usually to establish association, connections or relationships.

Review   Survey a topic, occurrence or idea, generally but critically.

State   Present the facts concisely and clearly.

Summarize State in concise form, omitting examples, analogies and details.

Trace   Follow the course, development or history of an occurrence, idea, etc.

However, notes can also be a crutch that guarantees not success, but audience boredom. You've probably seen any number of people get up in front of an audience and just read some papers they have in front of them. I guarantee you that, as a relative novice at public speaking, you will make one (and maybe all) of these "Big Three" mistakes if you bring your entire text with you:

- You will read from it, failing to make eye contact with your audience. This will help to ensure that you lose *their* interest and *your* credibility. How familiar can you be with a subject if you have to *read* your entire speech?

- If you stop reading for a second to ad lib or look at your listeners, you will lose your place. It's much harder to find that key word that will jog your memory on a full page of text than on an index card.

- You won't be familiar enough with your speech, because, after all, you'll have it there with you, so why bother rehearsing or memorizing anything?

Getting ready to get ready

Exactly what sort of talk is this going to be? Odds are, if you've been assigned to give a talk for a class, it will fall into one of the following categories:

- *Exposition*—a rather straightforward statement of facts.

- An *argument,* with which you are trying to change the opinions of at least a portion of the audience.

- A *description* that will provide a visual picture to your listeners.

- *Narration*—or storytelling.

The most common forms of oral reports assigned in school will be the exposition and argument. You'll find that you will research and organize your information for these types of speeches pretty much the way you would a term paper. So, review Chapter 8 (and, again, read *Write Papers*).

A note of caution: If you're preparing an *argument*, don't convince yourself you don't have to research *both* sides of the topic just because you're only presenting *one* of them. You should be doubly prepared with all the facts, as you might be challenged with questions or the arguments of other speakers.

As you gather information for your report, making notes on index cards as you did for your term paper, keep this in mind: In order for you to be effective, you must use some different techniques when you *tell* your story rather than *write* it. Here are a few:

- *Don't make your topic too broad.* This advice, offered for preparing written reports as well, is even more important when preparing a talk. Try giving an effective speech on "George Washington," "Hemingway's Novels" or "French Politics"...in 15 minutes, frequently the amount of time assigned for oral reports. These topics are more suited to a series of books!

  "George Washington's Effect on the Two-term Limit" or "The Imagery of 'The Old Man and The Sea'" or "The Rise of the Socialists in Post-War France" are more manageable. Narrowing the scope of

115

your talk will help you research and organize it more effectively.

- ***Don't overuse statistics.*** While they're very important for lending credibility to your position, too many will only weigh down your speech and bore your audience.

- ***Anecdotes add color and life to your talk.*** But use them sparingly, because they can slow down your speech. Get to the punch-line before the yawns start.

- ***Be careful with quotes.*** Unlike a term paper, a speech allows you to establish yourself as an authority with less fear of being accused of plagiarism. So you can present a lot more facts without attribution. (But you'd better have the sources in case you're asked about your facts.) You can use quotes, though, when they contain distinctive language or elicit an emotion. Be sure to attribute the source.

I've found that trying to shuffle a bunch of papers in front of a class is difficult and that note cards that fit in the palm of your hand are a lot easier to use. But only if the notes on them are very short and to the point, to act as "triggers" rather than verbatim cue cards—hanging on to 300 note cards is as difficult as a sheaf of papers.

Remember: You'll actually be holding these cards in your sweaty palms and speaking from them, so write *notes,* not whole sentences. The shorter the notes—and the more often you practice your report so each note triggers the right information—the more effective your report will be. (And the less you will have to look at them, making eye contact with your class and teacher easier.)

Here are some other ways to make your oral reports more effective:

- Pick out one person to talk to—preferably a friend, but any animated and/or interested person will do—and direct your talk to him or her.

- Practice, *practice, **practice*** your presentation. Jangled nerves are often the result of a lack of confidence. The more confident you are that you know your material, the less nervous you will be. And the better and more spontaneous your presentation will be.

- If you are like me and suffer from involuntary "shakes" at the mere thought of standing in front of a roomful of people, make sure you can use a lectern, desk or something to cling to.

- Take a deep breath before you go to the front of the class. And don't worry about pausing, even taking another deep breath or two, if you lose your place or find your confidence slipping away.

- If every trick in the world still doesn't steady you down, consider taking a public speaking course (Dale Carnegie, *et al),* joining the Toastmasters Club or seeking out similar extracurricular help.

Chapter Thirteen

WRITING WITH ADD

We both fear and pity kids on illegal drugs. But we also must face and deal with what's happening to the 3 million-plus who are on a *legal* drug—Ritalin, the prescribed drug of choice for kids diagnosed with Attention Deficit Disorder (ADD), hyperactivity or the combination of the two (ADHD).

I could write a book on ADD, which seems to be the "diagnosis of choice" for school kids these days. Luckily, I don't have to. Thom Hartmann has already written an excellent one— *Attention Deficit Disorder: A Different Perception*—from which I have freely and liberally borrowed (with his permission) for this chapter.

I'm going to leave others to debate whether ADD actually exists as a clearly definable illness, whether it's the "catchall" diagnosis of lazy doctors, whether teachers are labeling kids as

ADD to avoid taking responsibility for the students' poor learning skills, whether Ritalin is a miracle drug or one that is medicating creative kids into a conforming stupor.

All of these positions *have* been asserted, and, as hundreds of new kids are medicated every day, the debate about ADD is only likely to continue...and heat up.

That is not my concern in this book.

What I want to deal with here is the reality that many kids, however they're labeled, have severe problems in dealing with school as it usually exists. And to give them the advice they need—especially regarding note-taking—to contend with the symptoms that have acquired the label "ADD".

Some definitions, please

Just what is ADD? It's probably easiest to describe as a person's difficulty focusing on a simple thing for any significant period of time. People with ADD are described as easily distracted, impatient, impulsive and often seeking immediate gratification. They have poor listening skills and have trouble doing "boring" jobs (like sitting quietly in class or, as adults, balancing a checkbook). "Disorganized" and "messy" are words that also come up a lot.

Hyperactivity, on the other hand, is more clearly defined as restlessness, resulting in excessive activity. Hyperactives are usually described as having "ants in their pants." ADHD, the first category recognized in medicine some 75 years ago, is a combination of hyperactivity and ADD.)

According to the American Psychiatric Association, a person has ADHD if they meet eight or more of the following paraphrased criteria:

1. They can't remain seated if required to do so.
2. They are easily distracted by extraneous stimuli.

3. Focusing on a single task or play activity is difficult.

4. Frequently begin another activity without completing the first.

5. Fidgets or squirms (or feels restless mentally).

6. Can't (or doesn't want to) wait for his turn during group activities

7. Will often interrupt with an answer before a question is completed.

8. Has problems with chore or job follow-through

9. Can't play quietly easily.

10. Impulsively jumps into physically dangerous activities without weighing the consequences.

11. Easily loses things (pencils, tools, papers) necessary to complete school or work projects

12. Interrupts others inappropriately.

13. Talks impulsively or excessively.

14. Doesn't seem to listen when spoken to.

Three caveats to keep in mind: The behaviors must have started before age seven, not represent some other form of classifiable mental illness and occur more frequently than the average person of the same age.

Characteristics of people with ADD

Let's look at the characteristics generally ascribed to people with ADD in more detail:

Easily distracted—Since ADD people are constantly "scoping out" everything around them, focusing on a single item is difficult. Just try having a conversation with an ADD person while a television is on.

Short, but very intense, attention span—Though it can't be defined in terms of minutes or hours, anything an ADD person finds boring immediately loses their attention. Other projects may hold their rapt and extraordinarily intense attention for hours or days.

Disorganization—ADD children and adults are often chronically disorganized—their rooms are messy, their desk a shambles, their files incoherent. While people without ADD can certainly be equally messy and disorganized, they can usually find what they are looking for; ADDers *can't*.

Distortions of time-sense—ADDers have an exaggerated sense of urgency when they're working on something and an exaggerated sense of boredom when they have nothing interesting to do.

Difficulty following directions—A new theory on this aspect holds that ADDers have difficulty processing auditory or verbal information. A significant aspect of this difficulty is the very-common reports of parents of ADD kids who say their kids love to watch TV and hate to read.

Daydream—Or fall into depressions or mood-swings.

Take risks—ADDers seem to make faster decisions than non-ADDers. Which is why Thom Hartmann and Wilson Harrell, former publisher of *Inc.* magazine and author of ***For Entrepreneurs Only***, conclude that the vast majority of successful entrepreneurs probably have ADD! They call them "Hunters", as opposed to the more staid "Farmer" types.

Easily frustrated and impatient—ADDers do *not* beat around the bush or suffer fools gladly. They are direct and to-the-point. When things aren't working, "Do something!" is the ADD rallying cry, even if that something is a bad idea.

Why ADD kids have trouble in school

First and foremost, says Thom Hartmann, it's because schools are set up for "Farmers"—sit at a desk, do what you're told, watch and listen to the teacher. This is pure hell for the "Hunters" with ADD. The bigger the class size, the worse it becomes. Kids with ADD, remember, are easily distracted, easily bored, easily turned off, always ready to move on.

What should you look for in a school setting to make it more palatable to an ADD son or daughter? What can you do at home to help your child (or yourself)? Hartmann has some solid answers:

- *Learning needs to be project- and experience-based*, providing more opportunities for creativity and shorter and smaller "bites" of information. Many "gifted" programs offer exactly such opportunities. The problem for many kids with ADD is that they've spent years in non-gifted, Farmer-type classroom settings and may be labeled underachieving behavior problems, effectively shut out of the programs virtually designed for them! Many parents report that children diagnosed as ADD, who failed miserably in public school, thrived in private school. Hartmann attributes this to the smaller classrooms, more individual attention with specific goal-setting, project-based learning and similar methods common in such schools. These factors are just what make ADD kids thrive!

- *Create a weekly performance template* on which *both* teacher and parent chart the child's performance, positive and negative. "Creating such a larger-than-the-child system," claims Hartmann, "will help keep ADD children on task and on time.

- *Encourage special projects for extra credit*. Projects give ADDers the chance to learn in the mode that's most appropriate to them. They will also give such kids the chance to make up for the "boring" homework they sometimes simply can't make themselves do.

- *Stop labeling them "disordered"*—Kids react to labels, especially negative ones, even more than adults. Saying "you have a deficit and a disorder" may be more destructive than useful.

- *Think twice about medication,* but don't discard it as an option. Hartmann has a very real concern about the long-term side effects of the drugs normally prescribed for ADDers. He also notes that they may well be more at risk to be substance abusers as adults, so starting them on medication at a young age sends a very mixed message. On the other hand, if an ADD child cannot have his or her special needs met in the classroom, *not* medicating him or her may be a disaster. "The relatively unknown long-term risks of drug therapy," says Hartmann, "may be more than offset by the short-term benefits of improved classroom performance."

Specific suggestions about writing papers

- *Organize your time around tasks*—ADDers do well with short bursts of high-quality effort and attention. So the already-recommended notion of taking a paper and breaking it into a series of far-more-manageable steps—choose a topic, initiate library research, write first draft—is absolutely essential for ADDers. Such students might find it helpful to break even these steps into a great number of smaller, easily accomplished tasks—breaking "initial library research" into steps like 1) find pertinent books in card file; 2) find pertinent newspaper articles; 3) read and take notes on first book.

- **Break everything into specific goal units**—ADDers are very goal-oriented; as soon as they reach one, it's on to the next. So establishing *very* short-term, "bite-size" goals is essential. Make goals specific, definable and measurable. And stick to only one priority at a time.

- **Create distraction-free zones.** Henry David Thoreau (who evidently suffered from ADD, by the way) was so desperate to escape distraction he moved to isolated Walden Pond. Organize your time and workspace to create your own "Walden Pond", especially when you have to write. ADDers need silence, so consider the library. Another tip: Clean your work area thoroughly at the end of each day. This will minimize distractions as you try to write.

- **Train your attention span.** ADDers will probably never be able to train themselves to ignore distractions totally, but a variety of meditation techniques might help them stay focused longer.

INDEX